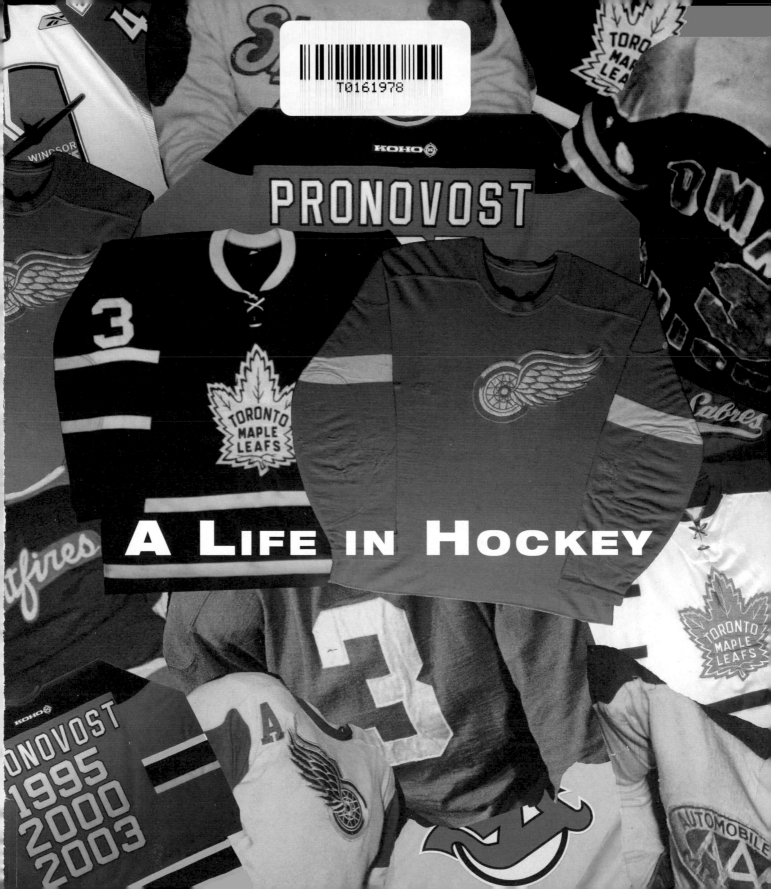

MARCEL PRONOVOST
A LIFE IN HOCKEY

with BOB DUFF

BIBLIOASIS

FIRST EDITION

Library and Archives Canada Cataloguing in Publication

Pronovost, Marcel, 1930-
        Marcel Pronovost : a life in hockey / Marcel Pronovost, Bob Duff.

ISBN 978-1-926845-98-2 (Red Wings)
        978-1-927428-24-5 (Maple Leafs)
        978-1-927428-06-1 (Hardcover)

1. Pronovost, Marcel, 1930-. 2. Hockey players--Canada--Biography.
3. Hockey scouts--Canada--Biography. I. Duff, Bob II. Title.

GV848.P77A3 2012   796.962092   C2012-901706-X

Edited by Dan Wells
Copy-edited by Tara Murphy
Typeset by Chris Andrechek

Canada Council for the Arts   Conseil des Arts du Canada   ONTARIO ARTS COUNCIL CONSEIL DES ARTS DE L'ONTARIO

Canadian Heritage   Patrimoine canadien

Biblioasis acknowledges the ongoing financial support of the Government of Canada through the Canada Council for the Arts, Canadian Heritage, the Canada Book Fund; and the Government of Ontario through the Ontario Arts Council.

PRINTED AND BOUND IN CANADA

Photo Credits:

Detroit Times archives: 61, 81, 126, 128, 130, 133, 136, 141, 142, 147; Dan Hamilton: 180; Hockey Hall Of Fame, Frank Prazak: 98; Dwayne LaBakas: 97, ,101, 103, 108, 149; Marcel Pronovost: 4, 6, 8, 9, 10, 12, 15, 16, 18, 20, 22, 24, 26, 27, 28, 30, 35, 36, 39, 40, 44, 47, 48, 50, 54, 56, 59, 62, 64, 67, 68, 70, 73, 74, 75, 76, 78, 79, 80, 84, 86, 89, 91, 93, 94, 109, 110, 114, 116, 119, 123, 125, 144, 152, 157, 160, 162, 163, 164, 166, 168, 170, 173, 177, 178, 181, 187, 188, 189, 190, 191, 192, 193, 194; RGB Photography: 105, 174, 184, 186, 193.

Contents

The Pronovosts pose for a family photo. Front row: my brother Jean, father Leo, mother Juliette and sister Nicole. Middle row: my brothers Andre, Benoit and Jacques and sister Monique. Back row: my brothers Claude and Gaston, me, and my brothers Roger and Rene. My sister Lily hadn't been born yet when this photo was taken.

LIFE IN SHAWINIGAN
GROWING UP AS PART OF A BIG FAMILY

SITTING IN THE SEATS AT WINDSOR ARENA, where I spent many a night scouring the ice surface below for National Hockey League prospects, it struck me almost as hard as those bodychecks I used to dish out for two decades as an NHL defenceman.

It was early in 2007. Both Windsor Arena and I had witnessed plenty of hockey. Windsor Arena was on its last legs, though—the new WFCU Centre would open its doors in a year's time—but yet, here I was, still going strong, 60 years after I first came to Windsor in pursuit of a career in the game that I love. It was my dream to make it in the NHL, but who would have guessed that it would become a career that would last a lifetime?

When you consider that I've spent the better part of my life working in professional hockey —65 years and counting since I first came to Windsor in the fall of 1947 to play junior for the Spitfires—it might come as a surprise to learn that, at first, hockey wasn't my winter sport. We skied. I was born by a golf course, so in the winter we did a lot of cross-country skiing.

It wasn't long, however, before hockey became my passion. Growing up in Shawinigan Falls, Quebec, the winters were long and harsh and provided the ideal combination for perfect hockey ice. I first put on a pair of skates when I was three years old. In Shawinigan Falls, it seemed as if every other house had a skating rink and there was also a massive outdoor rink right outside the school doors. We played hockey all day long. We'd run home from school at lunch and eat as fast as we could so we could get back to the ice for another game. We loved to play. Even after I turned professional in 1949, it was never about the money. It was always about the love of the game.

By the time I was five years old I was playing organized hockey. Like most kids I just sort of stumbled around the ice on my skates to start off, but it wasn't long before I caught on and caught up to the others on the ice. Naturally, most of the kids we played with were huge Montreal Canadiens fans, but surprisingly, I never was. Maybe I had an inkling of what my future held. Actually, I never really had a favourite NHL team as a youngster.

I was born in Lac La Tortue, Quebec, which is French for Turtle Lake. Today, it is one of the seven sectors that comprise the city of Shawinigan, but back then, it was a separate municipality. I was one of 12 children—eight brothers and three sisters. My mother Juliette came from a family of 16 kids, so she was used to being part of a big family. She was a very proud mom. Dad was a construction man. He worked in aluminum. Whenever he moved, we moved with him, but most of our lives were spent in Shawinigan.

Among the Pronovost children, Roger was the oldest, followed by Gaston. I was next in line, then Rene and Claude. Then came Monique, who broke the boy streak. Andre,

Arm in arm with my good friend and longtime teammate Johnny Wilson on Rankin Ave. in Windsor.

Benoit, Jacques and Nicole followed, then Jean. Liliane was the youngest.

I played left wing and centre as a youngster. I was a quiet-mannered, studious boy. Mostly, I minded my own business, though on the ice it could be a different story: even as a kid I cleaned a couple of clocks along the way. I remember my first serious hockey injury, when I got hurt during a game of shinny. I was playing with some of the neighbourhood kids on a frozen pond, and I ran into a high stick and ended up with a badly cut eye. I could have used a couple of stitches, but with 12 kids in our family we couldn't afford a doctor.

In competitive hockey, we played more or less town against town, and later parish against parish. We also played school hockey. I played for College Immaculate Conception Superior School (CIC). When Roger was on the intermediate team, I was good enough to move up and play with my oldest brother at a young age. I was the first one to do that, because I was a bigger kid.

As I got older, we started to ice some very impressive teams in Shawinigan. Both Shawinigan Tech and CIC, the latter operated by school sports director Brother Roger, were in contention annually for provincial crowns.

This young strapping lad would grow up to play 21 years as an NHL defenceman.

In 1944-45, we captured the Quebec provincial midget title. Over the years, I was fortunate to play in front of a number of future Hall of Fame goaltenders—Harry Lumley and Roger Crozier in Detroit, Glenn Hall in Windsor and Detroit, Terry Sawchuk in Windsor, Detroit and Toronto, and Johnny Bower in Toronto. But my first Hall of Fame goalie came that season with the Shawinigan midget club. Our goaltender was Jacques Plante.

We defeated Montreal's Notre Dame de Grace Royals 3-1 in the championship final on March 31, 1945. I started on left wing in the game. "CIC iced the same squad that lost to Park Extension in last year's final, with the exception of two boys," reported the April 2, 1945 edition of *The Montreal Gazette.* "They were the heaviest midget squad to be seen for some time and showed signs of excellent coaching. Goaler Plante gave a high-class display in the nets and looked like a real prospect."

I didn't play very long with Jacques, just that one season. Within two seasons, he'd jumped right up to senior hockey with the Shawinigan Cataractes of the QSHL. We didn't know at the time how good he'd turn out to be. During his career, Jacques won the Vezina Trophy seven times, and the Stanley Cup six times. He's also one of only six goalies to win the Hart Trophy as the NHL's most valuable player. We won the championship that year, beating Quebec in the semifinal and Montreal in the final, and Jacques was a big reason why we won.

The year after we won the midget title, my brother Rene was leading all scorers during the 1945-46 season in the bantam division with the Shawinigan Athletic Association. They finished first in their league and also won the provincial title with future New York Rangers goalie

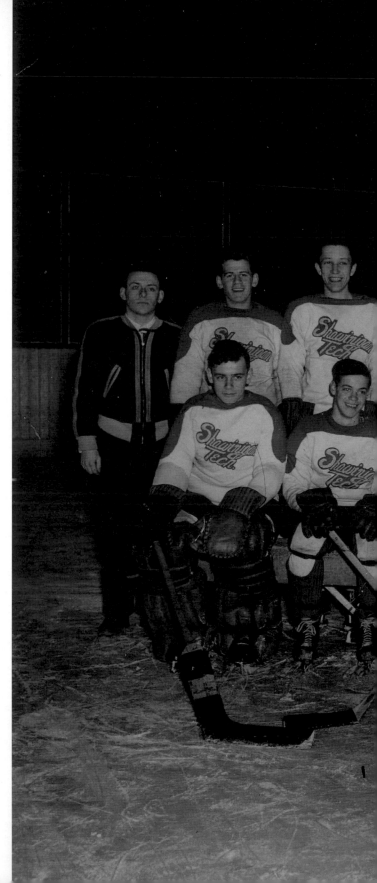

Shawinigan Tech Juvénile
1947-48

Gagné

My brother Rene was a teammate of Boom-Boom Geoffrion's on the Montreal Nationale juniors in 1950-51.

12

Marcel Paille between the pipes. A 3-3 tie was snapped when Rene buried the game-winner at 11:43 of the third period in the final, as SAA downed Montreal St. Malachie College 4-3.

Even though Jacques was gone, our winning ways continued. We won the Quebec juvenile title with Shawinigan Tech in 1946-47. During the playoffs, we beat Quebec City 7-1 in the semifinal and drubbed Sherbrooke 14-0 in the final. There were two other future NHLers, the Wilson brothers, Johnny and Larry, in our lineup. I played defence that season. We were

short on defencemen, and I was asked by the coaches to move back to the blue line. I didn't mind. I just wanted to play. And because of the skating and puck skills I'd developed as a forward, I was able to jump up and join the rush.

We were a powerhouse team and went undefeated through the exhibition, regular season and playoffs, allowing just six goals all season, while scoring 54. After winning our league title with a victory over Grand Mere, we drubbed Quebec 6-1 in the semifinal. I opened the scoring in that game.

In the championship game, on March 22, 1947, Johnny Wilson, who'd led Shawinigan Falls high school to a 4-0 victory over Granby in the provincial protestant schools' title match earlier that day with three goals and an assist, also led our rout with four goals and five assists. Larry Wilson added a goal and five assists, and I scored once and assisted twice from defence. My goal was the opener, making it the game-winner.

That was my first season playing along the blue line, and I turned some heads with my performance. "The defensive star of the game, and one to watch for the future was Marcel Pronovost, first string defenceman with the juvenile Cats," wrote Bill Gray. "This boy is a big 17-year-old youngster who is sure to go places. He clears and blocks very effectively and created a great impression with the fans when he scored his club's first goal after skating through the entire Sherbrooke squad to draw the netminder and sink the disc in the top corner for a picture goal."

Maybe it's not a surprise that we Pronovosts gravitated toward the rink, considering we had enough children at home to fill out two starting lineups. In fact, had we lived in a different era, I think we might have given the Sutter brothers a run for their money as far as how many of us could have been playing in the NHL.

Six Sutters—Brian, Darryl, Duane, Brent, Ron and Rich—played in the NHL between 1976-2001, and if our family had come of age during the height of NHL expansion, we might have had five brothers play in the league. As it was, I finished up as a Hall of Famer, while winning five Stanley Cups with Detroit (four) and Toronto (one). My brother Claude played goal for the Boston Bruins and Montreal Canadiens and Jean, my youngest brother, scored 391 goals for the Pittsburgh Penguins, Washington Capitals and Atlanta Flames between 1968-82. But there were more Pronovosts in elite hockey who didn't make the grade during the NHL's

six-team era. My oldest brother Roger won an intermediate championship in Shawinigan. Gaston, my second brother, won the Junior B championship. I won midget and juvenile championships. Rene, after me, won juvenile, midget and bantam titles. If we played today, there would have been at least a couple more of us in the big leagues.

Claude made his NHL debut on January 14, 1956. He played net for last-place Boston against Montreal, posting a 2-0 shutout win, and made 31 saves to make goals by Leo Boivin and Lorne Ferguson stand up for the victory. How he came to play that game is a strange story. Boston goalie Terry Sawchuk was out with a fractured finger. John Henderson was slated to play goal for the Bruins, and was recalled from Hershey of the American Hockey League. But some of Henderson's gear was lost in the transition to Montreal, including his size 14 skates, leaving the Bruins in a lurch.

At the time, Claude was the second-string goalie with the Montreal Royals of the Quebec Senior Hockey League and served as a practice goalie for the Canadiens in the days when NHL teams carried just one netminder. When Henderson couldn't play, Claude was sent over to the Bruins because of an NHL rule which required the home club to keep a spare goalie on hand in case he was needed by either team in an emergency.

Montreal coach Toe Blake explained how the scenario unfolded to the Associated Press. "He is our practice goalie and was in our dressing room when we told him he would have to play Saturday night," Blake said. "He looked at me and said, 'What's wrong with (Montreal goalie) Jacques (Plante)?' I told him nothing, but Pronovost was going to play for Boston. You should have seen the look on his face when he found out what he was going to do—play against us. He was stunned and got shaky. I guess he was afraid of what Montreal fans might do, but as it turned out, he didn't have a thing to worry about."

Claude's performance ended an eight-game losing streak for the Bruins. After the game, Boston coach Milt Schmidt asked if he could borrow Claude to play for the Bruins the next night against Toronto. Canadiens general manager Frank Selke Sr. said absolutely not, pointing out that Claude was Montreal property. The Bruins presented Claude with a crisp US $100 bill as payment for his work, as well as the No. 1 sweater he wore during the game and his goalie stick signed by the entire Boston

team. Selke made light of the loss, suggesting that, "Our players are such good sports, they hate to shoot hard against a sub goaler."

Leaving the rink that night, Claude hailed a taxi outside the Montreal Forum, asking the driver to take him to his home in the Montreal suburb of Beauharnois. Getting in, the driver asked Claude if he'd seen the game. "Yes sir," Claude answered. "I had a great seat. I could not have been closer to the action." Bemoaning the fate of his favoured Habs, the taxi driver lamented how it could be possible that the reigning Stanley Cup champions couldn't put a single puck past a bush-league netminder. "Who is this little brat who blanked the Canadiens for such a rotten club as Boston? Have you ever heard of him?" he asked Claude, still unaware of the identity of his passenger. "I know that he comes from Beauharnois," Claude said, smiling as he watched the cab driver's mind begin to decipher the situation. "But we are headed to Beauharnois," the cabby blurted out. Turning, he noticed a goalie stick next to Claude in the back seat of the taxi, the one the Bruins had signed for him. Suddenly, the taxi driver realized that Claude was indeed the man who'd stonewalled the mighty Canadiens, a certainty that was clinched when Claude offered to pay

14

In his NHL debut, my brother Claude filled in for Boston goalie Long John Henderson and shut out the Montreal Canadiens 2-0 at the Forum.

for his ride with the crisp American $100 bill that was his salary for the night. Proud to have driven the star of the night to his home, or perhaps simply looking to remove his foot from his mouth, the cab driver told Claude to keep his money. The ride was on him.

The funny thing was, the next day, we played the Canadiens and behind the goaltending of Glenn Hall the Wings also shut out the Habs 2-0. Afterward, reporters asked me about my brother's performance. "Claude is a fine goalie and this should do wonders for his confidence," I said. "Maybe now he'll get a break."

It's a tough memory, now, because I was so young. I took everything for granted at that age, as most of us do. As a goaltender, Claude, he was a Sawchuk type. He had a little bit of Glenn Hall and Sawchuk in his style.

As it turned out, Claude didn't get much more of a chance to play in the NHL. He appeared in two games for the Canadiens during the 1958-59 season. On February 5, 1959,

16

Three of the hockey-playing Pronovost clan. I'm on the left, Claude is in the middle and Roger, our oldest brother, is on the right.

Jacques Plante suffered a groin injury and gave way to Claude with the Leafs leading the Habs 4-1. Toronto finished with a 6-3 victory. Claude filled in again for an ailing Plante on March 19, 1959, once more against the Leafs. He allowed five goals in two periods and was replaced by Claude Cyr for the final frame of a 6-3 Maple Leafs victory.

Claude earned the nickname Suitcase because he played for so many teams during his career. He actually played in the Detroit system briefly during the 1956-57 season, when the Edmonton Flyers, the Red Wings' Western Hockey League affiliate, borrowed him from Montreal to fill in for Dennis Riggin, who had suffered strained back muscles in a game. Claude won the Quebec Hockey League's version of the Vezina Trophy during that 1958-59 campaign playing for the Montreal Royals, for whom he posted a 2.46 goals-against average with two shutouts, but it wasn't easy for even the elite goalies to find an NHL job in those days. There were only six up for grabs, and the guys who held them did all that they could to keep strangleholds on their positions.

Jean, he was a lot younger than I was. Jean was born in December of 1945, less than

two years before I left Shawinigan for good to play junior hockey in Windsor. Jean won a Memorial Cup with the Niagara Falls Flyers in 1964-65, but his big break came May 21, 1968, when his and John Arbour's contracts were sold by the talent-rich Boston Bruins to the expansion Penguins. He got to the NHL with Pittsburgh for the 1968-69 season, my last full season in the league, and we played four games against each other.

Our first meeting was a 2-2 tie at Maple Leaf Gardens on October 16, 1968. Jean assisted on Pittsburgh's second goal by Wally Boyer, but most people remember that as the game when Toronto defenceman Jim Dorey set an NHL record for most penalties (nine) and penalty minutes (48) in a game. To make it even more amazing, the game was Dorey's NHL debut.

We met again on November 20, 1968 and we whipped Jean's Penguins 5-2. I took a tripping penalty for upending my brother, but had the last laugh when my teammate Bob Pulford tied the game at 2-2 with a shorthanded goal while I sat in the penalty box. Jean assisted on Billy Dea's goal for Pittsburgh.

We blanked Jean and the Penguins 2-0 on January 25, 1969 behind the 30-save shutout goaltending of Bruce Gamble. In our final meeting on March 1, 1969, the Leafs roared out to a 3-0 lead on home ice, only to see the Penguins rally for a 3-3 tie. Jean started the comeback with a goal, but in our four games against each other, he never beat me. I was 2-0-2.

In 1972, when I was named coach of the Chicago Cougars in the fledgling World Hockey Association, I tried to sign Jean, whose contract was up with the Penguins. But on April 27, 1973, Jean re-signed with Pittsburgh, inking a multi-year deal. "I hope he isn't angry or disappointed, but this was a decision I had to make for myself," Jean told the *Pittsburgh Press* at the time.

Certainly, I understood. It would be tough on a player to be on a team with his older brother as a coach. Others would wonder if I was favouring Jean, and some might even think I would be harder on him than other players because he was my brother. "It would be tougher to play for my brother," Jean expressed. "To the other players, I would still be his brother. If he put me on the power play or gave me a lot of ice time, they might think it was because I was his brother."

Jean was a sensation in Pittsburgh. He scored 52 goals for the Penguins in 1975-76, and along with Pierre Larouche (53), became just the fourth set of teammates in NHL history to both produce 50-goal campaigns in the same season. Jean also topped the 40-goal plateau on three other occasions. He finished his NHL career having scored at least 20 times in 12 of 14 seasons. He set a Penguins record with 11 goals in March 1975 and during the 1975-76 campaign, played on the second-highest scoring line in the NHL with Syl Apps Jr., son of the longtime Maple Leafs captain, and Lowell MacDonald, who'd been my teammate

Jean, the youngest of the Pronovost brothers to make the NHL, was a 50-goal scorer for the Pittsburgh Penguins in 1975-76.

with Detroit in the 1960s. "I'm just lucky," Jean said humbly. "I guess I'm just in the right place at the right time."

Despite those numbers, and much like me, he often skated in the shadow of other more popular players. Jean was underrated, even though he was Pittsburgh's all-time goal-scoring leader. In 1975, Jean admitted as much to *Goal Magazine*. "The lack of publicity doesn't bother me," Jean said. "As long as my owners recognize me, as long as the general manager knows I'm doing the job, that's enough for me. I'm not a flashy-type player. I just go up and down my wing and do my job."

Marc Boileau, who'd been my teammate in Detroit in 1961-62, and coached Jean with Pittsburgh from 1973-76, seemed to understand Jean's value to the team. "Maybe people do underrate him, but we'll gladly keep him.

Maybe he's not noticeable out there because he just goes about his job, but you look at the statistics after each game and you'll see he's got a goal here, an assist there, a point here, a point there. I think Pronie belongs in the (Rick) Martin-(Guy) Lafleur class as a scoring wing. But no one says anything about him. He's taken for granted. He deserves a little more recognition."

Jean and I came close to becoming the first brothers to team up for 1,000 career NHL games each. I finished with 1,206 games, while Jean played 998. Russ (1,029) and Geoff (1,048) Courtnall would finally be the first siblings to achieve this feat in 1999.

The Pronovosts own a rich history in the NHL. And very soon, I would be leaving home, taking the next step toward becoming the first member of the family to get the chance to make that history.

19

Wearing my Windsor Hettche Spitfires team jacket. Note the patch on the arm that indicates we were IAHL champs in 1948-49.

TAKING UP A NEW POSITION
A SWITCH TO DEFENCE HELPS LEAD TO A PRO OPPORTUNITY

WHILE THE SHAWINIGAN TECH JUVENILES were plowing our way through the opposition during the 1946-47 season, the Wilson brothers were getting notice from National Hockey League clubs. The New York Rangers were scouting the brothers, as were the Montreal Canadiens, and it was expected that with their Quebec connection the Habs would win out and get their names on contracts.

In those days, NHL scouts relied heavily upon local arena managers to tip them off about prospects performing in their area. Marcel Cote was a Detroit Red Wings scout based in Quebec City who was advised to come take a look at the Wilson brothers. He watched them play for their Shawinigan Falls high school team in the afternoon, then decided to hang around until the evening and get another look at them in action as they played for the Shawinigan Tech juveniles.

After talking to the Wilsons following their high school contest, Larry Wilson advised Cote that there was another player on the Tech team that he should be considering. Larry said to him, "Go see this guy." That fellow was me. Cote ended up signing all three of us to C-forms, which were contracts prior to the days of the entry draft that tied an amateur player to a specific NHL club. From that point forward, all three of us would be property of the Detroit Red Wings.

The Wilsons and I, we all got to know each other and become friends while playing for Shawinigan Tech. We played on the same side starting in midget and we kept going. John was a year older at 18. Larry was 16 and I was 17. I think it helped, all of us coming to Windsor together, and then we had another fellow come along with us from Quebec, George Ouellette, who was from Mont Laurier.

As we got ready to head to Ontario in late August of 1947 for training camp and the pursuit of our dream, many of those closest to us came to see the three of us off. "John and Lawrence Wilson were fêted by their high school and Tech friends on Wednesday and Sunday prior to leaving for Windsor, Ont., where they will attend school and play for the Spitfires, entered in the Junior OHA," wrote the *Shawinigan Standard* on September 3, 1947. "Another outstanding member of the Tech Juveniles, Marcel Pronovost, will join the Wilsons at Windsor after training with Detroit in Waterloo, Ont."

At 16, I had been converted from forward to defence because of my size. I was a big scorer as a centre, but I played defence in 1946-47. I could play offence, I could play defence. Because of my skills as a forward, I was strong at rushing the puck up ice. On top of that, I was a strong skater. I was as quick as Bobby Hull. I could skate like the wind.

From where I was coming from it was a big jump going into the Ontario Hockey Association Junior A ranks, but I could skate, so it came easily because of that.

I started out the fall going to Detroit's main training camp in Galt, Ontario. I held my own there against those seasoned pros.

I wasn't intimidated. They put me out there and I rushed the puck. Go, go, go, go. I felt comfortable.

I started out with Leo Lamoureux as my defence partner. He was a veteran NHL player who had played 235 games with the Montreal Canadiens from 1941-47, winning a pair of Stanley Cups, but now, toward the end of his playing career, his rights belonged to the Red Wings. I learned a lot from him. He guided me through those first three years while I was trying to make the grade. It didn't take long for me to mature. I had to learn quickly.

Leo Lamoureux showed me the ropes as a young pro.

We actually had a lot in common. Like me, Leo had been converted from centre to defence early in his playing career. And though he wasn't born there, he ultimately made his home in Windsor, just as I would. Curiously, while I was making a name for myself in Windsor, Leo would head to my home area to take over as coach of the Shawinigan Cataractes of the Quebec Senior Hockey League from 1948-50. When Leo died at the age of 44 in 1961, Melvin T. Ross, the manager of the Indiana State Fair Coliseum—where Leo was coaching the Indianapolis Chiefs—donated the Leo T. Lamoureux Memorial Trophy in his memory. From 1961 until 2001 it was presented to the top scorer in the league. Leo is also enshrined in the Windsor Essex County Sports Hall of Fame, just like me.

The Red Wings had two camps. We had one camp in Winnipeg, then they took guys from Winnipeg and brought them into our camp in Galt. We came to Detroit about half-way through training camp.

Originally when I signed my C-form deal with the Red Wings, I was supposed to go to Galt, which was where Detroit's junior farm club was at the time. At the last minute, Lloyd Pollock and the Butcher brothers bought the club and moved it to Windsor. Lloyd Pollock became our manager and Jimmy Skinner became our coach.

Going to the Red Wings camp prepared me to play junior. Johnny Wilson was also ready though Larry wasn't quite ready yet. There were 4,100 packed into Windsor Arena on Friday, October 10, 1947, my first game for the Spitfires. We lost the pre-season game to the Omaha Knights of the United States Hockey League by a 5-2 count. Playing a team from our own league a week later, we swarmed the Toronto Marlboros 7-3 in another pre-season encounter.

Windsor Arena was a revelation. The shortness of the ice and the high boards really caught my attention. It looked as if they'd cut the end of the rink off to put in more seats, but I didn't mind that at all, because I was a hitter. The age of the old barn was another eye-opener. The building I played in in Shawinigan had been built in 1937, so it was quite new. I was a little bit spoiled. We also had to come down a flight of stairs from the dressing room to the ice surface, which was rather strange.

At the time, I never realized how many days and nights of my life would be spent inside the confines of Windsor Arena, as either a player, a coach or, for many years, a scout as well. To me, it was where I started on my way to a life in hockey, so in a sense, it was kind of like an old church. It was filled with hallowed memories, tradition. It fit like a comfortable old pair of shoes.

Windsor had the same fit for all three of us from Shawinigan. Shawinigan is a blue-collar, industrial town, and so is Windsor. We felt at home.

I remember one time the three of us were seated on a bench not far from the Ambassador Bridge on the Windsor side of the Canada-US border. And I remember looking across the river at Detroit and you could see the arena, Olympia Stadium, where the Red Wings

The Wilson brothers and I sit by the Detroit River, dreaming of playing for the Red Wings.

played, and I said to Johnny and Larry: "Do you think any of us will ever get there?"

Even though I was French-Canadian from Quebec, there wasn't a serious language barrier when I arrived in Windsor. Our family was bilingual. Mother was fluent in English because she worked as a maid, so she had to speak English with a lot of the people she worked for. The older kids, we picked up on it. We got to where we were speaking English pretty well, and I even went to an English school. We had English teachers. And mother always tested us in English.

Besides playing for the Spitfires, the Red Wings had another operation in place in the area that helped facilitate their dominance as an NHL power in the late 1940s and into the 1950s. The International Amateur Hockey League was a senior loop started after World War II, and it basically operated as a Detroit-run feeder system for the Red Wings. The majority of players in the league were already Detroit property, and the majority of the league's executive worked for the Red Wings organization.

What Red Wings' general manager Jack Adams did was split up the Spitfires junior players amongst the six IAHL franchises. For example,

Posing with George Rebstock, my Detroit Auto Club teammate in the IAHL.

28

in 1947-48 I was assigned to play for Detroit Auto Club while the Wilson brothers skated for the Windsor Hettche Spitfires alongside Gord Haidy and Glen Skov. The Giesebrecht brothers, Bruce and Bert, played for Detroit Metal Mouldings and Tom McGrattan and Doug McKay were with Detroit Bright's Goodyears. All of them would later play at least briefly in the NHL with the Red Wings. Spitfires GM Lloyd Pollock also operated the Hettche Spitfires franchise and Jimmy Skinner was the coach, so that was another connection.

It was a genius plan in terms of developing talent for the big club. I played 52 games during the 1947-48 season and an additional 51 during the 1948-49 campaign. We played a lot of games. You played in junior and the International League was as International as it got in those days. During the 1948-49 season, after Glen Skov suffered a knee injury, I was loaned in April to the Hettche Spitfires to play against the Spokane Flyers in the senior open division of the US Amateur Hockey Association championship. I don't know how they pulled that move off, because my addition to the Hettche Spitfires' roster added considerable power to Windsor's club both offensively and defensively. Games in the series were played at

Toledo, Windsor and Detroit. Spokane won the series in five games.

My first goal in Windsor came for Auto Club in my debut IAHL game. We whipped the Windsor Staffords 10-3 and the goal was reported in the local papers as "the highlight goal of the evening." I was hooked and spun around as I split the defence to get loose on a breakaway. Getting through the opening between the defence, I showed a great burst of drive when I came out of the spin still on my feet, picking up the puck to go right in on goalie Ken Freebairn to put the puck past him and into the net.

Meanwhile, in the junior ranks, the Spitfires were off to a 4-0 start behind the sensational goaltending of Terry Sawchuk, who had limited the opposition to just 11 goals

What's with the binoculars? Maybe I was doing a little birdwatching.

over those games. But our joy would be short-lived, because not long after the Red Wings announced that they were turning Sawchuk pro and assigning him to Omaha.

With Gord Buckley taking over between the posts we'd run it to 7-0 by the time I tallied my first goal in the junior ranks. It wasn't quite as spectacular as my first IAHL tally, coming as the 10th tally in 19-1 drubbing of the Toronto Young Rangers. Our line of the Wilson brothers with Gord Haidy combined for 18 points in that victory. After a couple of losses to the Oshawa Generals, Pollock brought in our third goalie of the season, handing the big stick to Ivan Walmsley.

Nothing seemed to slow us down, not even a two-month-long suspension of Skinner for an incident involving the game timekeeper and the officials in Barrie. We were playing in Galt against the Rockets on November 30, 1947. Near the end of the first period, Skinner went over to the penalty box, which was situated between the two benches and where the timekeeper sat. After a brief argument, Skinner took a poke at the timekeeper. Referee Jack McEachern came over to find out what was going on, also got into an argument with Jimmy, and Skinner swung at him as well.

Police were called in to subdue Jimmy and Spitfires manager Lloyd Pollock had to take over behind the bench for the rest of the game. We suffered a rare setback, losing 4-2.

Skinner was suspended indefinitely. He denied ever swinging at either person—he insisted he was just there to talk to Buck Houle, one of our defencemen, who was serving a penalty at the time, and that it was the timekeeper who came after him. After reviewing all the evidence, the Ontario Hockey Association didn't buy Jimmy's version of events and suspended him for 15 games.

Regardless, we finished first in the league with a 29-6-1 record. We topped the loop with 231 goals scored, but were only third-best in goals against, which would come back to haunt us in the playoffs.

With any championship team, you need the right people, the right chemistry and a few breaks. We had the right people. The only ingredient we were missing was goaltending. I tried to get Claude, my goaltender brother, to come to Windsor, but he wouldn't come. He feared that his English wasn't good enough. After Sawchuk left, we never really got settled in goal. If we'd had goaltending, we would have gone all the way.

29

Larry Wilson (16), myself (3), Johnny Wilson (15) and Bill Folk (2) with Indianapolis in 1950-51.

We got by our nemesis Oshawa in a six-game semifinal series and we jumped to a 2-0 lead in the final against Barrie. But the Flyers stormed back, thanks to some great goaltending from Gil Mayer, who posted two shutouts as Barrie won the next four games to take the series. We lost one game 10-0 and allowed 32 goals in the six games of the final series.

We should have won the Memorial Cup that spring. The five Stanley Cups I would later win with Detroit and Toronto never made up for that lost shot at the Memorial Cup. In junior, you don't have that much time to win it. That makes it special. We should have won it all that season. And if we could have had Sawchuk the whole year, we would have won it all.

That first year, I was a long way from home but the Windsor Spitfires hockey fans showed me kindnesses I'll always remember. They helped me with my English and encouraged me as a 17-year-old aiming for a hockey career.

Returning to Windsor again in the fall of 1948, just how much Sawchuk would have meant to us was emphasized when he was loaned to us for a pre-season game at Windsor Arena against Omaha. Sawchuk kept a clean sheet for two periods and we led 4-0. Passing the torch to Walmsley for the final frame,

Omaha beat him six times and rallied for a 6-5 victory. The contest was enlivened by a third-period brawl: one of the bouts consisted of me exchanging punches with Knights defenceman, and my future Detroit teammate, Bill Folk.

Our lineup for the 1948-49 season included the Wilson brothers, Glen Skov, Doug McKay and Jim (Red Eye) Hay, all future Red Wings. Our goalie, Dave O'Meara, was the son of sportswriter Baz O'Meara of the *Montreal Star*, whose claim to fame is that he was the one who handed Maurice Richard the nickname Rocket. Like me, he's in the Hockey Hall of Fame, inducted into the media wing in 1984.

We were riddled by injury during the 1948-49 campaign. Johnny Wilson fractured his collarbone. Ouellette tore up his knee. Skov broke his hand, McKay injured his ribs and I suffered a shoulder injury. I was hurt in a game at Toronto and up until then had been rendering great service both offensively and defensively. There's no doubt that my absence was felt.

Nonetheless, we stayed in the hunt for first place all season long, and in the end, finished on top for the second straight campaign with a 34-13-1 slate. We clinched top spot with a 4-2 victory over the Stratford Kroehlers on Feb. 13.

I assisted on a goal by Larry Wilson and also picked up a couple of penalties, including a 10-minute misconduct for disagreeing with the work of referee Perc Allen. In our final regular-season game, we edged the Toronto Marlboros 7-6. I went coast to coast during a two-man advantage to score what was described in the papers the next day as "the best goal of the night."

As a tune-up for the upcoming playoffs, an exhibition game was arranged between the Spitfires and the Detroit Red Wings. Imagine that happening today, a game between the Red Wings and the Spitfires, a junior-level team. No one would believe it.

The Red Wings crossed the border to Windsor Arena for the showdown on Feb. 19, 1949. The Windsor Junior Hockey League was the benefactor of the exhibition game and $1,300 was raised via gate receipts from a crowd of 2,170.

The Wings, who were in first place in the NHL, showed up armed to the hilt. Harry Lumley started in goal, while (Black) Jack Stewart, Red Kelly and Bill Quackenbush patrolled the blue line. The forward unit that opened the game was Detroit's vaunted Production Line of Sid Abel, Gordie Howe and Ted Lindsay. We were all thrilled to play against Gordie.

In an effort to even matters out, the Wings loaned defenceman Lee Fogolin Sr. and centre George Gee to us for the night. It seemed to be making a difference when I set the pro-Spitfires crowd abuzz, burying the rebound of a Larry Wilson shot to put Windsor in front at 7:37 of the opening frame. Before the period was over though, Howe tallied twice and the Wings carried a 2-1 advantage to the dressing room.

When Howe completed his hat-trick in the second period, it appeared as if the rout might be on until John Taylor pulled one back for us to narrow the margin to 3-2 after 40 minutes. Abel and Bud Poile scored quickly in the third period to make it 5-2 Detroit, but if people thought the game was over they were dead wrong. Johnny Wilson narrowed the gap to 5-3, beating Detroit backup goalie Jim Shirley on a penalty shot.

Within three minutes, we'd tied the score on goals by Gee and Johnny Wilson. Finally, with 5:45 left in the game, Abel dented the twine for the game-winner, allowing the Wings to escape with a hard-fought 6-5 decision. "This was as good a workout as we've had in a long time," Detroit coach Tommy Ivan

34

said after the game. "It's the best possible tune-up for our OHA playoffs," suggested Skinner. In his column the next day, Doug Vaughn of *The Windsor Star* noted that Detroit GM Jack Adams, watching from the press box, "was particularly pleased with the impressive showing of what he knows will be several of his Red Wings stars of the future—fellows like Marcel Pronovost, the Giesebrecht brothers, Bert and Bruce and the other set of brothers, Larry and John Wilson. He was rooting for them all the way and if he had been equipped with a megaphone, you could have heard him yelling instructions all over the rink."

In the OHA Junior A playoff system employed during this time, the first and second-place teams would meet in a best-of-seven set, with the winner going directly into the final series. We were paired up with the Barrie Flyers, the same team that had eliminated us in the final the previous spring. And this spring, it turned out even worse for us. We were swept in four straight, dropping 6-3, 5-4, 7-0 and 7-4 setbacks. Just like that, the promise was gone, our season over.

But my season didn't end. The Red Wings recalled 10 players as insurance for the upcoming Stanley Cup playoffs. They added Fred Glover, Nels Podolsky, Calum MacKay, Gerry Reid, Sawchuk and Ben Woit from Indianapolis of the American Hockey League, Sam Mulholland from Philadelphia of the AHL, Gordie Bell and Jim Uniac from Omaha of the United States Hockey League, and me from the Spitfires. I was the only amateur player among the 10 recalled. I didn't get to see any action, but travelled with the team as the Wings lost the Stanley Cup final to Toronto. It was my first taste of real NHL action, albeit as a spectator.

The move to Windsor had paid off. I was a well-groomed young player, ready to take the next step into professional hockey. Coming to Windsor to play for the Spitfires was the best thing that ever happened to me. Windsor was the right place for me to be at the right time in my life. Boy, did I ever get to play a lot of hockey while I was there.

I still remember my mother years later, saying to me, "Marcel, what would you have done if we hadn't given you permission to leave?"

"I would've gone anyway." I told her. "You wouldn't have been able to hold me back with a pair of wild horses."

"That's what I thought," she said.

Wearing No. 8 in action for the Detroit Auto Club against the Windsor Hettche Spirfires in an IAHL game at Windsor Arena.

In the uniform of the USHL's Omaha Knights, my first pro team. Notice that I'm wearing No. 3, which would become my trademark number.

A STIRRING DEBUT
AN INJURY TO GORDIE HOWE OPENS THE DOOR TO THE NHL

AS TRAINING CAMP OPENED for the 1949-50 season, I felt that I was ready for the next step up the hockey ladder and the Red Wings agreed with me. Even though I was only 18 and still had another year of junior eligibility, they opted to sign me to a contract and turn me professional.

The Red Wings assigned me to the Omaha Knights of the United States Hockey League, the same team where they'd assigned Terry Sawchuk two years earlier when both of us were 17-year-old rookies with the Windsor Spitfires. Detroit had two minor professional farm clubs in those days—the Indianapolis Capitols of the American Hockey League, which was one step below the NHL, and the Omaha club, which was the next level down the ladder.

You might not think of a town in Nebraska as a hockey hotbed, but Omaha, it had a hockey tradition. The farm club for Detroit was there, and it had been there for years. It was the city where Gordie Howe began his pro career in 1945. We played at the Ak-Sar-Ben Arena, which a lot of people don't realize is actually Nebraska spelled backwards.

The coach in Omaha was Mud Bruneteau, who holds legendary status in Red Wings lore. As a rookie during the 1935-36 season, Bruneteau had scored after 176 minutes and 30 seconds of play to give the Wings a 1-0 victory in their Stanley Cup semifinal opener against the Montreal Maroons, ending what remains the longest game in NHL playoff history. It was a great debut for him in the Stanley Cup playoffs, and it also launched Detroit en route to the first Stanley Cup ever won by the franchise. Bruneteau scored that goal against Lorne Chabot and during the 1949-50 USHL season, Lorne's son Lorne Chabot Jr. played goal for the Tulsa Oilers.

Bruneteau was also part of three brother combinations who were with Omaha that season. His younger brother Eddie played for the Knights. The other two were sets of rookies who, like me, had graduated from the Spitfires—Bert and Bruce Giesebrecht and my Shawinigan pals the Wilson brothers, Johnny and Larry.

Omaha was a good place for me to be at that time in my career. I learned a lot in Windsor and I got more tutoring when I played in Omaha. It wasn't like a lower minor pro league of today, where the other players would all be from your peer group, young kids just up from junior or college hockey. The USHL was loaded with players with an NHL pedigree. Eddie Bruneteau had played 180 games for the Red Wings from 1940-49 and was a 17-goal scorer during the 1945-46 campaign.

Every roster in the league was littered with grizzled NHL veterans. Many had made the grade during World War II, when so many NHLers were enlisted in the war effort, but now that the pros were back from military service they'd been farmed out.

The Kansas City Mohawks, a Chicago feeder club, suited up former Black Hawks like goalie Sugar Jim Henry, defenceman Doug Baldwin and forwards Hank Blade and Adam Brown, the latter a two-time 20-goal scorer in the NHL with Detroit. The Louisville Blades had defenceman Harry Dick (Chicago), goalie Gordie Bell (Toronto Maple Leafs) and

forward Joe Bell (New York Rangers). The Tulsa Oilers trotted out ex-Boston Bruin Lloyd Gronsdahl and former Montreal Canadien Marcel Dheere. The Saint Paul Saints were led by forward Clint Smith, who won the Stanley Cup with the Rangers in 1939-40 and was a two-time Lady Byng Trophy winner. The Saints also had former Bruin Gino Rozzini and ex-Rangers Bob Dill, Jack Lancien, Scotty Cameron, Hub Anslow, Lin Bend and Lloyd Ailsby. The Minneapolis Millers came at you with forward Walt Atanas, an ex-Ranger, and defenceman Johnny Mariucci, one of the first prominent American-born players in the NHL, who had played for Chicago in the 1940s.

Both Mariucci and Dill came had reputations as tough guys from their NHL days. In Minneapolis, when you played against Mariucci, he was tough, but Dill he just thought he was tough. One night in Omaha, Pete Durham, one of our other defencemen, who ended up leading the league that season with 193 penalty minutes, cleaned Dill's clock.

We opened the season with a 5-0 whitewash of the Louisville Blades and four of the five goals were scored by guys who'd played junior in Windsor. The Giesebrecht brothers each scored once, as did Francis O'Grady. And the other scorer? Yours truly. We were all making our professional debuts, and we all celebrating by lighting the lamp behind the net.

About a month into the season, we really got things rolling and people around the hockey world started to notice of the depth within the Red Wings organization. "Jolly Jawn Adams, major domo of the far-flung Detroit hockey domain, is viewing the world through rose-coloured glasses these days," wrote Doug Vaughan. "The Red Wings are so far in front in the National League that the rest of the clubs need field glasses to see them. Omaha Knights, featuring such ex-members of the Windsor Spitfires as Larry and John Wilson, Bert and Bruce Giesebrecht, Marcel Pronovost and Francis O'Grady, are currently setting the United States League on fire after getting off to a slow start."

OMAHA KNIGHTS
1949-1950

FRONT ROW, left to right: Marcel Pronovost, Larry Wilson, Frank O'Grady, Manager Harry Fowler, Bill Brennan, Coach Mud Bruneteau, Hartley McLeod, John Wilson and Bill Folk. SECOND ROW, left to right: Trainer Charlie Homenuk, Eddir Bruneteau, Motto McLean, Keith Burgess, Bruce Giesebrecht, Bert Giesebrecht, Sam Mulholland, Jake Forbes and Publicity Director Bernard Kelly. REAR ROW: Peter Durham and Gordon Heale.

I'm wearing a worried look as I help defend the Omaha goal, which is under attack from the Kansas City Mohawks.

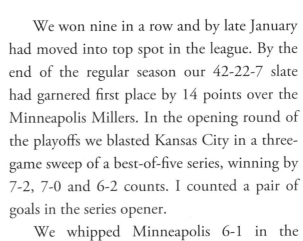

We won nine in a row and by late January had moved into top spot in the league. By the end of the regular season our 42-22-7 slate had garnered first place by 14 points over the Minneapolis Millers. In the opening round of the playoffs we blasted Kansas City in a three-game sweep of a best-of-five series, winning by 7-2, 7-0 and 6-2 counts. I counted a pair of goals in the series opener.

We whipped Minneapolis 6-1 in the opener of the league final. I figured in three of the goals with assists. I set up Larry Wilson to give us the lead in Game 2, and Keith Burgess made it 2-0, but it was all downhill after that and Minneapolis evened the series, drubbing us 7-3.

It was a sign of things to come. Minneapolis whacked us 5-1 in Game 3. We were just over two minutes away from elimination in Game 4 when, at 17:50 of the third period, Larry Wilson and I combined to create a goal for Johnny Wilson and tie the score 3-3. But it was all for naught when Bill Richardson scored at 9:37 of overtime to give the Millers a 4-3 win and the league title.

There was a lot of speculation about who would be rookie of the year in the USHL and Bill Brennan, our goalie in Omaha, who'd led the league with 41 wins, was getting a lot of the attention. But on March 28, 1950, I was named rookie of year. In 69 games I produced 13 goals and 39 assists for 52 points, setting a USHL record for defencemen. I'd also collected 100 penalty minutes. I was the first defenceman ever to win the award, the same trophy Sawchuk had won two seasons earlier. I was pleased to win, because let's face it, I had a lot of competition. Besides Brennan, there were the two Wilsons as well, just on my own team.

I polled 19 of a possible 25 points in the voting for the award. Lorne Ferguson of Tulsa, later my teammate in Detroit, finished second with 13 points and John Wilson was third with eight points.

As well, I was named to the First All-Star Team of USHL. Even though we'd finished first, I was the only Omaha player to garner First Team status, and I did so by polling the most votes of any player, 23 out of a possible 25 points. It paid off for me, too. I received a $250 bonus for earning rookie of the year and an additional $200 bonus for my All-Star selection.

That alone would have made for a successful launch to my pro career, but the best was yet to come. The day before Omaha's final game of the playoffs against Minneapolis, the Red Wings, who'd lost Howe to a serious head injury in their Stanley Cup opener against the Leafs, and then Jimmy Peters to a twisted knee, recalled former Spitfire Gord Haidy from Indianapolis. There were rumours of more recalls to come.

Newspapers were reporting the possibility that a trio of other ex-Windsor Spitfires may be promoted to the Red Wings for the fifth game of the series in Detroit. That trio ended up being the Wilsons and I. The word was that we'd be recalled as soon as the USHL playoffs were done. There was even speculation that I might be moved up to right wing to take Howe's spot on the Production Line.

We lost to Minneapolis the next night and the three of us got the call to report to Detroit immediately. A lot of people ask me if I was surprised to be called up from two leagues below the NHL to skate in the Stanley Cup playoffs without a game of NHL experience, but to tell the truth, I wasn't shocked at all. I was a confident kid. When I signed my C-form contract with Detroit in 1947, I figured, "I'm there." Indianapolis, they were in the playoffs in the AHL, so it made sense the the big club would call on us.

42

Gerry (Doc) Couture filled in for Howe on the Production Line next to Sid Abel and Ted Lindsay until Game 4 of the semifinal series against Toronto. Then Red Kelly moved up from defence to right wing. Clare Martin played defence in Game 4 in Kelly's spot.

The Wilsons and I, all three of us played Game 5 of the series, a 2-0 loss that left the Wings down 3-2 in series. Detroit dressed five defencemen for that game—Jack Stewart, Leo Reise, Lee Fogolin, Clare Martin and myself.

"The freewheeling Pronovost was by far the most effective of the trio," *The Windsor Star* noted of my NHL debut. "He was used considerably on defence and looked good in handing out stiff bodychecks and leading several rushes."

We rallied for a 4-0 whitewash of the Leafs in Game 6 at Maple Leaf Gardens, staving off elimination and forcing a decisive seventh game back at Olympia Stadium. It was a tremendously tough series. Lindsay and Toronto's Bill Ezinicki were going at it every game. We went into overtime in Game 7 deadlocked in a scoreless draw when my defence partner Leo Reise tallied to give us the win and move the Wings into the Stanley Cup final for the third season in a row.

Despite my youth and inexperience, Detroit coach Tommy Ivan wasn't afraid to utilize me. I saw a lot of ice time in both games, as both a defenceman and a forward. Both my puck-carrying skills and my defensive work received praise.

The Wings had a young nucleus then—players like Howe, Kelly, and Lindsay were all in their early- to mid-20s—and it was apparent that more young talent was about to explode on the scene.

"The freewheeling Pronovost appears to be in the Big Time to stay," *Windsor Star* columnist Doug Vaughan wrote. "In the three games he played against the Leafs, the 19-year-old youngster handled himself like a veteran."

The Toronto writers, getting a look at me for the first time, were amazed at my poise, polish and speed. Said one writer who has been covering NHL games for 20 years: "There's a kid who can't miss. He simply oozes colour and has everything needed to go with it. I predict that he will be an outstanding star before some of the writers around the league find out how to spell his name correctly."

It was lavish praise indeed for a young fellow who might have still been playing junior hockey, and was only one year removed from the amateur ranks. But as nice as it was to hear such talk, I tried not to think about it, instead focusing on the task that lay ahead of us.

The Wings were listed as 12-5 favourites to win the Stanley Cup. We would be facing the New York Rangers in the final. No one had expected the fourth-place Rangers to get the better of the second-place Montreal Canadiens in the other semifinal series, but as I always say, there is a big difference between what you expect and what actually happens. Just look at the 2012 playoffs, or just about any other play-off year, for that matter.

A lot of people seriously doubted the Rangers' chances of beating us because they'd have no home-ice advantage for the final. The circus had moved into Madison Square Garden, so Games 2 and 3 of the series would be played in Toronto and the rest of the games on our home ice at the Olympia. During the regular season that might have mattered, but in the playoffs, especially in the final series, home ice means very little. There's too much at stake.

We learned quickly just how tough it was going to be when we lost Lindsay to a back injury prior to Game 1. Suddenly, two-thirds of our vaunted Production Line was out of action.

I'm in the big time with the Detroit Red Wings.

Regardless, we posted a solid 4-1 victory over the Rangers in Game 1 and it was a big night for me. I assisted on Doc Couture's goal, our fourth of the night, for my first point in Stanley Cup action, and my first point as an NHLer for that matter.

I used my speed and drove down the left wing, then zipped a perfect pass across to Couture, who was lurking at the side of the Ranger cage to bat it in for an easy goal. It seemed as if I was fitting into my role as a big-league player almost seamlessly.

44

I felt better and more comfortable every time out. I could move the puck out of my own team's end of the rink with a smoothness that many veteran NHL defencemen couldn't match. Once under a full head of steam, I was mighty hard to stop. The Rangers found this out and no less than three of them drew penalties trying to stop me in Game 1 of the final series.

Going to Toronto for Game 2, the tables turned and the Rangers whipped us 3-1. Suddenly, the Wings were contemplating a shakeup in the lineup for Game 3.

After the Game 2 loss, Detroit general manager Jack Adams said the team intended to sit out Pete Babando, Larry Wilson, Steve Black and myself. Inserted into action were going to be Al Dewsbury, Doug McKay, and Gord Haidy all up from Indianapolis, where they had just won the AHL Calder Cup championship, as well as Jimmy Peters, whose knee ailment had healed sufficiently enough for him to return to action.

This knee-jerk reaction to one loss was panned by the critics, who felt that it was too much of a sweeping change for a single loss. Removing me from the lineup was strongly questioned by reporters covering the series, who felt that I'd done well in the three games I'd played against the Leafs and had been equally effective in the two games with the Rangers.

The argument for the change put forth by the Wings was that Dewsbury was a more experienced performer and thus less likely to make a major error on the ice that would cost the team in a key moment of a game. It was a logical argument, and in Game 2 of the final series I did have a couple of defensive lapses, which, admittedly, could have been costly. But they were no worse than some of the mistakes made by vastly more experienced members of the team.

Ultimately, the Detroit brain trust reconsidered, keeping me in the lineup while opting to sit out Martin. We won 4-0 to take a 2-1 edge in the best-of-seven set. I saw brief action in the second period, but was mostly welded to the bench during the course of the game.

The Rangers weren't ready to roll over, and in fact won the next two games, taking 4-3 and 2-1 overtime decisions to gain a 3-2 series lead, thanks to a pair of overtime goals by Rangers forward Don (Bones) Raleigh. One more win by New York and the Wings would lose in the Stanley Cup final for the third spring in a row.

Down in the series 3-2, we had a big meeting in Toledo, where we stayed during the playoffs. Jack Stewart was one of our alternate captains. Sid Abel was his roommate, and Jack, he tore him a new one. (Don) Bones Raleigh, he was Sid's check. Jack looked sternly at Sid and said, "Don Raleigh is making a fool out of you." I remember that Sid later told me: "I was afraid to go to bed that night."

Instead, Sid woke up. Abel scored two goals in Detroit's 5-4 Game 6 victory and once more, we would go to a decisive seventh game. We fell behind 2-0 and 3-2 in Game 7, but we came back and ousted them 4-3 in overtime. Pete Babando scored the Cup winner from a faceoff in the Rangers' zone, an opportunity I had helped to create. I'd just come off the ice. I made the play to throw the puck in their end and we went in to freeze it for the faceoff.

George Gee beat the Rangers' Buddy O'Connor on the draw. Babando whipped a backhander that found its way through a maze of legs and sticks and into the far corner of the net behind a screened Charlie Rayner in the New York goal. Babando scored two goals in the game—his only two goals the entire playoffs.

It was quite a whirlwind for me. I played the last nine games and that's how I got my name on the Cup the first time. Three of us on that team—Haidy, McKay and I—all won the Cup before we'd ever played a regular-season NHL game. Amazingly, it would be the only game either of them would play in the NHL, while I'd go on to play 21 years in the league.

It was all like a dream. There I was sipping champagne at Detroit's Book Cadillac Hotel at our victory party. At night, looking back, I was glad that I signed with Detroit. I was confident in my abilities and when Adams signed me to a C-form, that was it as far as I was concerned. I had their eye. Sure, I was cocky. But I wasn't really shocked to be there so young, not really, because that's the goal I'd had. Still, I was glad, because the Wings had put their faith in me and I wanted to prove them right.

Players who won the Stanley Cup before playing a regular-season NHL Game

Jimmy Franks, Detroit 1937

Earl Robertson, Detroit 1937

Paul Goodman, Chicago 1938

Gaye Stewart, Toronto 1942

Les Costello, Toronto 1948

Phil Samis, Toronto 1948

Gord Haidy, Detroit 1950

Doug McKay, Detroit 1950

Marcel Pronovost, Detroit 1950

Doug Anderson, Montreal 1953

Ab McDonald, Montreal 1958

Bill Hicke, Montreal 1959

Wayne Hillman, Chicago 1961

Chico Maki, Chicago 1961

Milan Marcetta, Toronto 1967

Lucien Grenier, Montreal 1969

Danny Schock, Boston 1970

Chris Hayes, Boston 1972

Bruce Cowick, Philadelphia 1974

Brian Engblom, Montreal 1977

Pierre Mondou, Montreal 1977

Kelly Buchberger, Edmonton 1987

Mike Needham, Pittsburgh 1992

Steve Brule, New Jersey 2000

Ryan Carter, Anaheim 2007

Drew Miller, Anaheim 2007

Hoisting coach Tommy Ivan up on my shoulders as we revel in our 1953-54 Stanley Cup triumph.

DETROIT DYNASTY
MY STANLEY CUPS WITH THE RED WINGS

THE CELEBRATION HAD BARELY DIED DOWN from our 1949-50 Stanley Cup win when I headed home to Shawinigan, only to discover there was another party waiting. On May 21, 1950, I was honoured at a reunion of College Immaculate Conception Superior School, where I'd attended school and played hockey, winning the 1944-45 Quebec provincial midget title.

Once I returned to Detroit in the fall, I was quick to discover that the Wings had big plans for me, and were proclaiming I would make great strides as an NHL player. "Jack Adams never speaks disparagingly of one of his hockey players until he has dealt him off to some other club, which is certainly good business," wrote Dink Carroll in the *Montreal Gazette*. "On the contrary, he pulls out all the stops in describing their abilities as long as they are with him. Thus, Marcel Pronovost is the league's new colour guy, a fellow who breaks like a shot and is something of a cross between Eddie Shore and Kenny Reardon."

Things were going well for me in training camp until one day in practice, when I made one of my patented rushes up the ice with the puck and tried to split the defensive pair of Leo Reise and Bob Goldham. They caught me in a sandwich and that's when I broke my cheekbone.

Even after that, though the injury slowed we down a little bit for a couple of weeks, both Detroit coach Tommy Ivan and GM Jack Adams told me that they were still high on my abilities and both remained confident that I would make the grade that fall as an NHL regular.

I kept playing with my broken cheekbone and then in an exhibition game against the Sault Ste. Marie Greyhounds got hit with a shot and broke a bone in my ankle. I kept playing on it, because I didn't want to get sent down to Indianapolis, but my play struggled because of the accumulated injuries.

After a weekend series with the Montreal Canadiens in early December, *Montreal Gazette* writer Dink Carroll was critical of my work. "Marcel Pronovost, Detroit's rookie rearguard termed 'a second Eddie Shore' by Jack Adams, played briefly in the final period. The boy can skate, but he gets too many useless penalties at this stage of his development."

A couple of days later, on December 5, 1950, Clare (Rags) Raglan was recalled from Indianapolis and I was assigned there. "Pronovost...was one of the Red Wings' brightest rookies last season, but has not been able to match that form this year," noted the Associated Press. "Red Wings officials said he would get more work with Indianapolis and expressed belief that this would be for his own good."

I wasn't happy to go down—what player would be?—but I made the best of it. I averaged nearly a point per game with the Capitols, producing 9-23-32 numbers in 34 games, and the Red Wings took notice. In mid-February, they called me back up to the big team and Raglan and I changed places again. They sent Rags down because he couldn't skate like I could.

The time in the minor leagues did me good. My injuries healed and I regained

Playing for Indianapolis in the AHL, I'm in alone on Pittsburgh goalie Gil Mayer, but this time, he foils me with a poke check.

Playing for Indianapolis in the AHL, I'm in alone on Pittsburgh goalie Gil Mayer, but this time, he foils me with a poke check.

the form that I'd displayed during the 1950 Stanley Cup playoffs, and had caused so many observers of the game to predict that I was headed for a spectacular career in the National Hockey League. While I was in Indianapolis, I was a big factor in the Caps' rise from last place to the runner-up spot in the Western Division of the American Hockey League.

I was barely 20 years old, but for the remainder of my 21-year NHL career, I'd never be assigned to the minor leagues again. People think that's a big deal, but you can't be proud of that, because it has been accomplished by a lot of people.

I came back up for a 2-1 victory over the Habs as we spoiled Rocket Richard Night at the Forum. In my second game back I really made a big splash. Trailing the Boston Bruins 2-1, I beat Bruins goalie Jack Gelineau for the tying goal with just 42 seconds left to play for my first NHL goal. I'd gone scoreless in my previous 21 games with the big club that season.

The goal came from a pileup in front of the Bruin goal. Gordie Howe and Sid Abel assisted on my tally. We looked to be headed for just our fourth loss in 30 games on Olympia ice,

as Boston carefully nursed its one-goal lead, checking us to a standstill.

The one-minute-to-go warning had been announced over the public address system when I came hurtling out of the Detroit zone and passed to Abel in centre ice. Abel relayed the disc to Howe, who drove to the goal-mouth, where he was knocked down by Boston defenceman Bill Quackenbush. A pileup ensued.

Boston goalie Jack Gelineau was on his hands and knees searching for the loose puck. So was another Bruins defender, their captain Milt Schmidt. Abel took a swipe at the bobbling puck and missed. I rushed in and took another swing and didn't miss. The puck went through Abel's legs and into the cage.

We finished first in the NHL again that season with a 44-13-13 record, but our joy was short-lived, for we were upset by third-place Montreal in the opening round of the playoffs. I got a surprise at the end of the season when I was named to the American Hockey League's Second All-Star Team, even though I'd only played 34 games for Indianapolis.

Early in the 1951-52 season, I got another pleasant surprise when on October 23, 1951, the Red Wings played an exhibition game in Shawinigan against the Cataractes, a Detroit farm club, winning 7-2. Before the game, Jean Landry, the Shawinigan Tech hockey coach when Larry and Johnny Wilson and I played for the team, presented us all with pen and pencil sets. Larry Wilson, who was celebrating his 21st birthday, also received a basket of fruit from the local A&P, where he'd worked while living in Shawinigan.

I started on defence with Ben Woit. Terry Sawchuk got the start in goal, with Tony

Leswick and the Wilsons on the forward line. Leswick quickly opened the scoring on a pass from Larry. Metro Prystai and Gordie Howe each scored twice, while Marty Pavelich and Johnny Wilson added singles. Sawchuk played the first period, then gave way to Lefty Wilson. Both goals for Shawinigan were scored by my former Windsor Spitfires teammate Georges Ouellette against Lefty Wilson. Afterward, the team attended a dinner sponsored by the

HOW WINGS SALVAGE TIE IN LAST MINUTE OF PLAY

Detroit Times Photo

This is the way the Red Wings managed to tie Boston, 2-2. Capt. Sid Abel of Wings (third from right) is shown battling for loose puck as Milt Schmidt (third from left) on ice tries to tie up disc. Abel freed the puck to Marcel Pronovost at his right, who shot through Abel's legs into net behind goalie Jack Gelineau. Woody Dumart (14), Murray Henderson and Gordie Howe (on the ice) watch the play.

Rookie's Late Score Saves Wings

This mad scramble led to my first NHL goal. I'm about to backhand a shot through the legs of our captain Sid Abel and past Boston goalie Jack Gelineau to earn Detroit a 2-2 tie with 42 seconds left to play.

The only outdoor game of my NHL career was played at a prison. On Feb. 2, 1954 when we played the inmates at Marquette, Mich. prison. I'm standing just behind coach Tommy Ivan.

teaching staff of the Shawinigan Technical Institute on behalf of myself and the Wilsons.

We opened the NHL regular season with a 1-0 shutout of the Boston Bruins, which was a sign of things to come during what would be a magical season. It was the 13th straight season the Wings opened with a win or a tie.

We got on a roll and never looked back. We won five of our first six games and lost just two of our first 18. Over 70 regular-season games, we lost back-to-back games on only one occasion. But the best was yet to come.

Finishing first, we drew Toronto in the opening round of the playoffs. Starting at the Olympia, we blanked them 3-0 and 1-0. Moving to Maple Leaf Gardens, we completed the sweep via 6-1 and 3-2 triumphs. Then we sat back and rested while Montreal and Boston duked it out in the other semifinal.

The Canadiens eventually won that series in six games and we opened the final round at the Montreal Forum. We shut down their attack and got enough goals to win 2-1 and 3-1 decisions. Back on home ice, we were once more perfect, recording consecutive 3-0 shut-outs, and the Stanley Cup was ours for the second time in three springs. In accepting the Cup from NHL president Clarence Campbell, our captain Sid Abel said, "Thanks for the return of the Stanley Cup. Now it's back in Detroit, where it belongs."

As Game 4 wound down, something was tossed from the Olympia seats and landed on the ice. Linesman George Hayes went over to see what it was and you should have seen him jump back. So I decided to take a look. I smacked it with my stick. Right away, I knew what it was, and I knew that it was dead. It was an octopus. I scooped it up and skated over to the penalty box with it, but nobody there wanted to touch it, either. I didn't think about it, I just picked it up. Oh yeah, you better believe I wondered why they were throwing the octopus on the ice.

Decades later, the octopus has become a Red Wings tradition, almost as well known as the winged wheel itself. Its origins stemmed from two Detroit fishmongers, Jerry and Pete Cusimano, who were also Red Wings season-ticket holders. They knew that the Wings were going for a record that night, the first team ever to sweep to the Cup in eight straight games, and since an octopus has eight tentacles, they felt it was the perfect symbol for the perfect team.

As far as I'm concerned, that 1951-52 Red Wings club was the best team ever assembled.

The 1951-52 Cup champion Wings were the first NHL team to go 8-0 in the playoffs. I'm the back row, next to Gordie Howe.

The youngest and the best. Only four of our players—forwards Abel and Leswick and defencemen Reise and Goldham—were over the age of 26. Sure, it may be hard to judge that for yourself when you are right in the midst of the team, but do the math and you'll see where I am coming from. Eight straight wins with four shutouts and only five goals against in those eight games, it makes for a pretty good argument.

You used to almost feel sorry for the teams that we played next after any of our rare losses, because you just knew we were going to kick the stuffing out of them.

Others agreed with me. "This Detroit club is one of the best-balanced, if not the very best, I have ever seen," noted vanquished Montreal GM Frank Selke. "It is solid all the way."

That team had everything going for it. In goal, Sawchuk delivered a performance for the ages. His four shutouts tied Dave Kerr of the 1939-40 New York Rangers and Frank McCool of the 1944-45 Leafs for the most in one playoff year. He was so hard to beat that spring that one writer suggested Sawchuk performed as if he were triplets.

You want to talk depth? Consider that Howe, who led the NHL with a club-record

47 goals that season, didn't even score until the sixth game of the playoffs, and yet we were still unbeaten. He and Lindsay finished 1-2 in NHL scoring that season. Howe also won the Hart Trophy as MVP of the NHL to go along with his Art Ross Trophy as scoring champ. We posted a .714 winning percentage and led the NHL with 215 goals. On defence, both Kelly and I were headed toward Hall of Fame careers. And Sawchuk won the Vezina Trophy as the NHL's top goaltender, posting 12 shutouts, with a league-low 1.33 goals against. Right-winger Howe, left-winger Lindsay, Sawchuk and defenceman Red Kelly were all selected to the NHL's First All-Star Team.

That team had a little bit of everything. We had talent with guys like Howe and Kelly, we had a great goalie in Sawchuk, we had tough-ness—nobody wanted to mess with Howe and Lindsay. I was a great hitter. And guys like Glen Skov and Pavelich and Leswick were great checkers. But in or out of the dressing room, everyone stood on equal footing. There were no egos. We were all close friends.

What I remember most about that team wasn't all the wins or the silverware we earned, but how we were as a unit. We bonded together and were a close-knit bunch. There

was camaraderie. We all got along with each other. We liked being around each other. We did a lot of train travel and after the games, we'd always gather and have a discussion of what went on and what was causing problems. It helped you get prepared for the next game.

Off the ice, we also did a lot of activities as a group, including a Monday night bowling league. The captains—Goldham, Kelly, Howe and Lindsay—they picked the teams and we put up $1,000 for the winning team, so it was fun and competitive. We ran it just like the NHL and we allowed trades. It turned out that Jack Adams was one of the worst bowlers, so he got traded a lot. I think the players got a real kick out of that.

A couple of times a month, the guys would all get together and go out on the town and the married players would bring their wives. We socialized as a group. The fact that we spent so much time together away from the rink and had a genuine fondness for each other, I think it showed up on the ice.

A tribute to the hockey minds that com-prised that team was that nine of us—Lindsay, Kelly, Alex Delvecchio, Abel, Fred Glover, Vic Stasiuk, the Wilson brothers—would all later serve as coaches or GMs in the NHL.

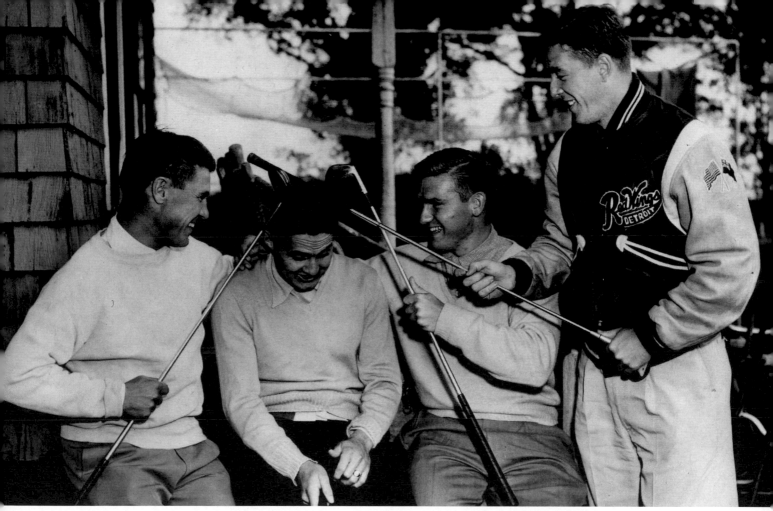

You could say that Tony Leswick, Johnny Wilson and I are ironing out our differences with Earl (Dutch) Reibel on the golf course.

And what was even more impressive was that we turned in that rock-solid defensive performance while missing both Leo Reise (badly cut boot) and Red Kelly (sprained left hand) from our blue line for periods of time during the playoff run. I was the one who injured Leo. I collided with him during practice and my skate punctured his left ankle, lacerating it. He was out 8-10 days. Kelly was already out with an arm injury suffered in the semifinal versus Toronto. The team called up Hughey Coflin,

who'd played for Indianapolis, but the Capitols had already been eliminated from the playoffs, so he had to fly in from his home in Blaine Lake, Saskatchewan. Goldham and I logged a lot of ice time in those playoffs, as did Ben Woit. And Kelly was able to play some minutes despite his injury.

It turned out we had more than enough to get the job done. The last team to go unbeaten in an entire playoff year was the 1928-29 Bruins, but they only required five wins to capture the Stanley Cup. "You've just seen the best-balanced club it has ever been my privilege to watch, mine or anyone else's, in my 35 years in hockey," Adams claimed.

"They are the grandest bunch of fellows I ever hope to be associated with. They all played wonderfully well but in almost every game our scoring punch was provided by a different line or a different individual," added Detroit coach Tommy Ivan.

Even Campbell was full of praise. "We are honouring a team which has set records which may never be equaled," he said while presenting the Cup to our team.

If you want to know the key to our success, it was scouting. We had an experienced guy in Carson Cooper, who'd played in the NHL in the 1920s and 1930s. He unearthed quite a few exceptional players. Among Cooper's finds were Lindsay and Kelly.

Manitoba scout Bob Kinnear found Sawchuk and in Saskatchewan, Fred Pinckney was responsible for discovering Howe. Marcel Cote, Detroit's Quebec scout, came up with the Wilson brothers and me.

Together, they found all the required ingredients for a championship club—solid defence, great scoring with players like Abel, Howe and Lindsay, and grinders who did the dirty work. Metro Prystai scored two goals in Game 4 against Montreal and Leswick and Pavelich completely smothered Canadiens star Rocket Richard, who was held without a goal the entire series. And let me tell you, that was no easy feat.

People today don't know what competitiveness is. A guy like Lindsay would carve your eyes out. He was an aggravating, irritating presence. He was such a fiery type that they actually had to revise the public address system at Olympia Stadium. The fellow who announced the goals and penalties was situated near the penalty box, but his microphone would pick up Lindsay's words—a combination of English and profanity—whenever he was penalized and broadcast it to a shocked crowd.

In 1951, Lindsay and Boston's Bill Ezinicki, who were both undersized wingers who played the game with the temperament of heavyweights, engaged in a fight so vicious that Ezinicki was left with a broken nose and 19 stitches in his face. Their battle lasted three minutes and officials couldn't get them separated. So appalled was Campbell by the display that he suspended both from participating in the remaining games between the two teams that season.

No one played with the snarl of Ted Lindsay. He's so mad here that he's just thrown his stick at Boston defenceman Allan Stanley.

It was said that the nastiest words that you could utter in one of the other five NHL rinks in those days were Ted Lindsay. Gordie Howe once said that Lindsay was so mean that as a kid he had to keep a pork chop in his pocket just to get the family dog to play with him.

Terrible Ted fought anyone and everyone —opponents, teammates who foolishly crossed his path during practice, referees, league officials, even his own coaches and managers.

Lindsay hated to lose so much I think he would have fought his own mother on the ice if he thought it would give his team a chance at victory.

He played the game the only way he believed it should be played—with the utmost passion and while skating along a thin line between the laws of the game and the laws of the street. He instinctively despised anyone who stood in his way. He always said he hated everyone he played and they all hated him. He wouldn't socialize with anyone in the league who wasn't a Red Wing, not even at the NHL All-Star Game.

As far as I'm concerned, there were only two players who had everything that you would want in a hockey player—Lindsay and the Rocket. They never took a night off. There is not one hockey player—today, yesterday and maybe even tomorrow—that could electrify a crowd the way the Rocket could. He had that uncanny sense and whether it was in Montreal, Chicago, New York, or anywhere else, he could grab that puck and bring 20,000 people out of their seats. But it seemed he always saved his best games for Detroit.

Sharing a moment with Ted Lindsay in the Detroit dressing room. You wouldn't get this close to him on the ice without feeling some pain, though.

When he crossed that red line and approached the blue line, you could see the glimmer in his eyes. No one drove to the net like him. The Rocket didn't just want to put the puck into the net. He wanted to put it through the net. He was spectacular and he never missed the net. He could be on his knees, he could be on his back, he could be on his can, but the shot was on the net. He had only one thing in mind when he got the puck. He was going to the net and he was going strong.

The Rocket, he didn't like me too much, because I'd hit him and I'd hit him hard. I was one of the few guys he couldn't knock off his feet, who could match his strength. He and I had a few run-ins. He hated my guts, but I wouldn't fight him, because there was no point. Why take a chance at losing? I wasn't that good at it. But I could keep him upset and hopping mad another way—by checking him. He tried to go through me, over me, under me, around me, but I could skate with him and he'd end up on his butt. So then he tried to intimidate me, but I couldn't be intimidated. I wasn't fun to run into. One time, I broke his little brother Henri's wrist, and the Rocket, he didn't like that at all.

The Rocket, he ran me with a high stick and knocked out two of my teeth. Adams accused

him of deliberately trying to injure me. "He's full of baloney," The Rocket said. "I hate that club. I just got mad and took a run at everybody. But I didn't mean to hurt them. I have nothing against Pronovost—he's a regular guy. I ran into him and I'm not sure what hit him."

I wasn't dirty too often, but when I snapped Henri Richard's wrist, I took a good crack at it. I got a major for it. Another time, I got Montreal's Dickie Moore in the boards, because he'd taken me into the boards, and I broke his wrist. I stood over him and said, "Now, that's payback." There was a lot of payback in those days. You saw each other so much and spent so much time battling each other on the ice, it was hard not to develop very strong feelings.

I remember one time Doug Mohns put me through the end boards in Boston. We came back and played the next night in Detroit and I got him cornered with my defence partner Larry Hillman. Larry went like this, I went like that, and we went boom. You paid back. Toronto captain Ted Kennedy, I owed him one for years. I finally got a hold of him one game, and Toronto defenceman Tim Horton grabbed me from the back. Timmy and I, we had an affinity. He'd come in and restrain his

63

guy and I'd come in and restrain my guy. This time, he grabbed me in a bear hug and he said, "That's enough, Marc. That's enough." I was after Ted Kennedy for a little bit of a payback for something he'd done to me.

A lot happened between teams in those days when you were playing each other 14 times a year. These guys today don't know what it's like to play seven games in nine nights. Those back-to-back games? They were like one 120-minute game with four points at stake. They were not for the faint-hearted. If you gave someone the lumber one night, he'd give it right back to you the next. You had to play 14 games against the guy, so there was toughness, but there wasn't as much spearing and stick work. Now you may see a guy in October and won't play him again until March.

You didn't talk to the opposition during the season in those days. On those weekends when you would play back-to-back games against the same team, opposing players would occasionally meet at the train station after the game en route to the rematch. You'd be waiting together for the same train but at opposite ends of the platform. And if you wanted to go to the dining car to get something to eat, you waited until the train pulled into a station, got

Giving it my best shot in an attempt to put the puck past Montreal goalie Gerry McNeil.

off and walked down the platform to the dining car. There was no way you were going to go through the car where the other team was sitting to get to the food. If there was any contact at all, it was no more than a passing nod, even between childhood friends. There were no friends during hockey season, only teammates and opponents.

The Detroit roster underwent some significant changes prior to the start of the 1952-53 season. Sid Abel left to become player-coach of the Chicago Black Hawks and Reise was dealt to the Rangers for Reg Sinclair. The season opened with Sinclair in place of Abel between Howe and Lindsay on the Production Line, while Lindsay succeeded Abel as captain. Sinclair was the only player in our opening-night lineup who wasn't a Red Wing in 1951-52.

We beat the Rangers 5-3 in our season opener at Olympia Stadium, extending a home-ice season-opening win streak that stretched all the way back to 1938. But our season didn't get off to a great start. We were 4-6-3 in early November, including a 9-0 loss in Montreal where everything went wrong. Montreal wouldn't let us have the puck all night long. Within 10 minutes, we were down 5-0 and it went downhill from there.

I was particularly embarrassed, because this was the first hockey game that my mother had ever agreed to come to see. After the first 10 minutes, she asked the usher to give her a chair and she went and sat in the hallway, because she was afraid that there were going to be a lot of fights because the game was out of hand.

We were served a piece of humble pie, but that's probably what turned the season around for us. A 15-game unbeaten run through the month of December righted our ship. "Detroit is still the team to beat," Canadiens coach Dick Irvin proclaimed.

We finished on top of the standings again with a 36-16-18 slate and opened the playoffs with a rousing 7-0 drubbing of Boston. Then the Bruins rattled off three straight wins. We rallied to take Game 5 by a 6-4 count, but Boston took Game 6 by a 4-2 margin, and just like that, we were out of the playoffs, no longer Stanley Cup champions. We'd allowed 21 goals in six games, which isn't the type of defence that wins titles.

We returned in the fall of 1953 with renewed vigor and purpose, once again racing to a first-place finish during the regular season, an eventful one for me. In November, I suffered

66

My dad Leo and mom Juliette came to Detroit to check me out in action.

I donned this football facemask after fracturing my cheekbone in training camp
with the Red Wings in 1950.

a sprained ankle and missed five games. Later in the season, I was sprawled on the ice in front of the Detroit net during a wild scramble when my good friend Sawchuk, attempting to clear a rebound away from his net, swung his stick, missed the loose puck, but connected solidly with my forehead and opened a large gash. You can still see the scar from where I got the stitches.

My worst injury of that campaign came, of all places, in Omaha, where I'd launched my pro career back in 1949. The Chicago Black Hawks weren't drawing very well and switched some of their games to neutral sites, including a game with us on February 25, 1954. During the game, I hurt my back and later it was discovered that I'd fractured a vertebrae. I missed most of the remaining regular-season games before returning for the playoffs, but I was playing in considerable pain.

I wasn't too worried about it. My game is a contact sport. It's a game of men. I expected to get bounced and get my lumps. I also expected to play in every single game. Hurt or not, you had to be ready to play every night. If you weren't ready you played in the American League. The whole point is this: If I went out on the ice and thought I wasn't

going to get hurt, I just wouldn't have been a hockey player.

Injuries were part of the game. During my playing days, my medical report included a broken jaw, seven smashed teeth, a hernia, a damaged Adam's apple, a hemorrhaged eyeball, two broken wrists, elbow chips, a severed cheek vein, separated shoulders, and a concussion. I also broke my nose 14 times.

I was chasing a loose puck one night. My stick got jammed between the boards and I basically speared myself in the groin. That's when I got the hernia. The doctors wanted to operate at the time, but I wouldn't have it. I wore a goalkeeper's jockstrap over the injury and kept on playing. I had the operation when the season was over.

As for the vertebrae injury, there was even a positive outcome to the layoff. While recuperating, I'd often skate alone at the Olympia, still wearing my neck harness. There wasn't much that I could do, so I'd practice my long shots for five minutes every day, working at hitting the empty net. Wouldn't you know it, during Game 3 of our Stanley Cup semifinal series against the Toronto Maple Leafs, we were up 2-1 late in the game when Leafs' coach King Clancy pulled goalie Harry Lumley for an extra attacker. The puck came to me and I drilled it into the centre of the Leafs' net from 110 feet away. All that practice paid dividends.

We whipped Toronto in a five-game semifinal and would meet the Montreal Canadiens in the Cup final series for the second time in three springs. It was a real back-and-forth series. We took a 3-1 lead, but like the old saying goes, the hardest game to win in any series is the last one. Montreal won Game 5 by a 1-0 count in Detroit, then whipped us 4-1 back at the Forum and we were coming back to Olympia Stadium for a decisive Game 7.

I played in Game 7s of the final series four times, which is a Stanley Cup record. This would be my second one, and the second one that would go to overtime, also a Stanley Cup mark. In fact, there's only ever been two Stanley Cup finals to go seven games and to have Game 7 decided in overtime.

Floyd Curry gave Montreal a 1-0 first-period lead, but Kelly tied it for us in the second

Skating away after the handshakes following our victory over Toronto in the 1956 Stanley Cup semifinals.

period. After a scoreless third frame, it was on to OT. Early in the extra period, Leswick lofted a shot from well out at the Montreal goal. Canadiens goalie Gerry McNeil drew a bead on it, but at the last moment, Montreal defenceman Doug Harvey tried to catch the puck and it deflected off his glove, over McNeil's shoulder and into the net at 4:29 of the first overtime. The Cup was ours once more.

There's nothing more nerve-wracking than playing in overtime in Game 7 of the Cup final series. It certainly does feel tense. Every move you make, the game, the season, depends on it, so you've got to be careful. I was the one who put the puck into the New York Rangers' zone for the faceoff that led to our game-winning goal in overtime during Game 7 of the 1950 final series and that's a memory I'll always treasure. When the game ends and you're on the right side of the outcome, there's just so much emotion. It's a sense of satisfaction more than relief. The beer tastes better, I can tell you that. Another thing I can tell you is that our celebrations were nothing like they are today, where every player gets his day with the Cup. We'd go back to the Sheraton-Cadillac Hotel in Detroit for a party and that would be it until next year.

We won that spring because we had talent, but also because we had heart. There was a lot of character in that Detroit dressing room and it showed when it mattered most. The next day, many were offering opinions that it was the best playoff series they'd ever witnessed. And while Leswick was the ultimate hero, with a little bit of luck I could have saved us all the trouble of dealing with the intensity that comes with a Game 7 overtime.

In the first five minutes of the game, I made a rush down the left-wing side and around Harvey and blasted the rubber into McNeil's pads from the short side. Eight minutes later, I used my speed to bullet my way down the centre of the ice. It looked as if I would try to split the Montreal defence of Harvey and Dollard St. Laurent. The Hab defenders were so sure of what I was going to do that they rammed together like a couple of runaway freight trains and went down in a heap. Meanwhile, I freewheeled my way past them, cutting to the right side of Harvey to go right in on the Montreal goal. Once again, McNeil came up with a fine save. I tried for the short side of the net and the Montreal goalie kicked the shot out with his right pad as he fell the other way.

We came back in the fall determined to ensure that there would be no letdown like there was following our 1952 Cup win, but the Canadiens seemed to have other ideas. They jumped ahead in the standings and led the league for most of the season. We were 10 points behind Montreal with 10 games to go and then we got on an incredible roll, winning our last six in a row and losing just twice in our last 22 games.

When we came to Montreal to play the Canadiens in the second-last game of the season on March 17, 1955—St. Patrick's Day—we were just two points out of a first-place tie with the Habs.

It wasn't uncommon for the visiting team to be in for a rough night when they played at the Montreal Forum in the 1950s. But I have to admit, the Wings were even more hesitant upon their arrival that night. Just two days earlier, NHL president Clarence Campbell had suspended Rocket Richard for the remainder of the regular season and playoffs for his role in a brawl at Boston.

The Wings would be the next team to play in Montreal and considering we were battling the Habs for first place, people anticipated there would be trouble at the game. There was a feeling before the game that something could happen. By the time the game started,

an unruly mob of some 6,000 had gathered on the street outside the rink. Although advised to stay home, Campbell arrived and took his usual seat in the Forum stands.

Campbell endured eggs and four-letter words tossed in his direction, but with Detroit leading 4-1 after 20 minutes, the trouble began to escalate. We were in our dressing room for the intermission, but we could hear a lot of noise, so we had a feeling something was going on, but we didn't know what. I remember our coach Jimmy Skinner looking at his watch and thinking the intermission was running too long.

Just then the two GMs, Adams and Frank Selke of Montreal, came into the room and told us someone had thrown a bomb into the rink and the game had been forfeited to us. They told us to stay put until somebody came to get us. Smoke started seeping into the room under the dressing-room door. We took some wet towels and jammed them under the door so the smoke couldn't get in.

Not long after, police and arena security staff came to get the Wings, slipping us out the back entrance to a waiting bus. We were taken to our hotel and then to the train station, where we departed for Detroit. We missed the

Tangling for space in front of the Montreal net with Canadiens' Norris Trophy-winning defenceman Doug Harvey.

whole thing. We didn't know about the riot until the next day.

As the crowd spilled out of the rink on to Ste-Catherine Street, the mob began smashing windows and looting stores. By the time order had been restored, some $50,000 in damages had been inflicted and 52 people were arrested.

The league awarded us a 4-1 victory by forfeit. In our final game of the season, we whipped

Watching with a big smile on my face as our play-by-play broadcaster Budd Lynch is about to sip from the Stanley Cup in 1950.

the Canadiens 6-0 at Olympia Stadium to clinch first place for a record seventh season in succession, a mark that's never been matched in NHL history.

With Richard suspended for the remainder of the campaign, we went on to win the Stanley Cup. It was a goaltenders' series with Terry Sawchuk versus Montreal's Jacques Plante, my old Shawinigan teammate. They won their three games at home and we won our four, so that home-ice advantage we earned by finishing first proved invaluable.

I only collected three points the entire playoff—one goal and two assists—but my last helper was a big one. I set up Gordie Howe in Game 7 for the Cup-winning tally. There was just 11 seconds left in the second period when Howe made it 2-0 in a game we'd win 3-1. I set it up when I grabbed the puck just inside the blue line on the left boards and relayed it to Howe, who came tearing in with Floyd Curry trying to check him. Howe got his stick on the puck and flipped it into the net.

I'd been in the NHL six seasons and had won four Stanley Cups. It was getting to be habit-forming, but little did I know that it was a habit that was about to be broken.

Players Who Won Four Stanley Cups With Detroit

Marcel Pronovost (1950-52-54-55)

Gordie Howe (1950-52-54-55)

Red Kelly (1950-52-54-55)

Ted Lindsay (1950-52-54-55)

Marty Pavelich (1950-52-54-55)

Johnny Wilson (1950-52-54-55)

Kris Draper (1997-98; 2002-08)

Tomas Holmstrom (1997-98; 2002-08)

Nicklas Lidstrom (1997-98; 2002-08)

Kirk Maltby (1997-98; 2002-08)

Darren McCarty (1997-98; 2002-08)

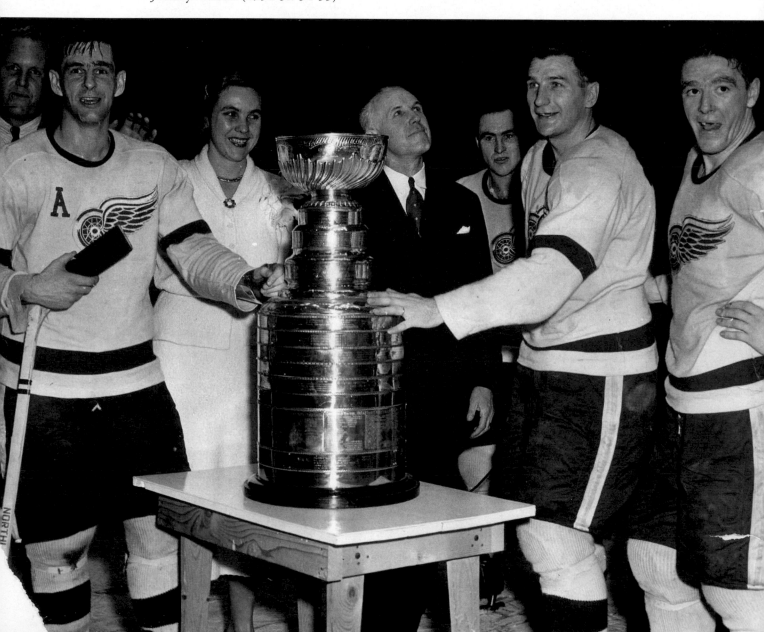

We were a new-look club to start the 1955-56 season. Nine of our players from the 1955 Cup-winning team were dealt away in the summer. Among the newcomers were three future Hall of Famers – goalie Glenn Hall and forwards John Bucyk (first from left in second row) and Norm Ullman (middle of third row). I'm fourth from the left in the back row, next to Red Kelly.

WEARERS OF THE WINGED WHEEL
MEMORIES OF MY DETROIT YEARS

WHEN PEOPLE ASK ME ABOUT those glory years in Detroit, it's easy to reminisce. It seems like it was yesterday. At least that's the way it feels to me. There were so many memories, so many happy moments. Winning four Stanley Cups in six years, you get used to that and you enjoy it. Those were good times. You think that they're never going to end, and why would you when you take a look at the Red Wings lineup in those days?

I was one of six Hall of Famers on that 1955 Stanley Cup championship team, along with Gordie Howe, Ted Lindsay, Terry Sawchuk, Alex Delvecchio and Red Kelly. You start in goal with Sawchuk, whom I still believe to this day was the best that ever was to play the position. On defence, besides me, we had Kelly. Red was an all-around hockey player. He could play forward. He could play defence. There was only one flaw: he wasn't a hitter. But you have to have all kinds on a hockey club. He had me to do the hitting. He's a hell of a guy, Red Kelly. While he was playing in Toronto, he went into politics and served for a time as a Canadian member of parliament. He was also extremely successful in business.

Delvecchio was young at the time, but he grew into a leadership role and became captain of Detroit for over a decade. He was so relaxed and low key. Nothing bothered him. People think of him as a passer first, but he scored a lot of big goals. He was a little bit of both, in my opinion. I give him credit. He could put the puck in the net.

I've spoken before about Lindsay and how I feel he was as competitive a hockey player as there was. I remember when they brought him back to Detroit, out of retirement after four years, and he signed with the Wings in 1964. I knew that if they had a chance, they would go fishing for talent. He'd been out of the game for a few years, but he hadn't lost any of his fire.

Maybe this version of the Production Line—Ted Lindsay, Gordie Howe and Alex Delvecchio—could have also been dubbed the El Producto Line—considering the stogies they are lighting up. The funny thing is, none of them were smokers.

And he still had the big guy, Gordie Howe, on his line.

He worked on left wing on the Production Line with Howe and Sid Abel, and that forward line, it was unbelievable. Sid, he was up in age, but he was the mentor to the other two guys. He had the young Lindsay and the young Howe.

After he retired, Sid became coach of the Red Wings during the 1957-58 season, replacing Jimmy Skinner. Even though I'd played with Sid, you got used to seeing Sid behind the bench. He was certainly there for a long time. Sid had the same temperament as a forward that he had as a coach. But he never played defence.

As a player, Sid was a gentleman. On a Detroit team with so many young players, he was the mentor, a father figure. He had a way of making you feel like every night was just another game and you could go out there and have some fun together.

Behind the bench, Sid was the best guy that I ever worked for. He understood hockey players and was always good to me. His theory of coaching was similar. During an era when bench bosses like Montreal's Toe Blake, Toronto's Punch Imlach and Phil Watson of the New York Rangers would drive their players to the point of breaking, Sid operated differently. Instead of practicing us hard after a tough loss, he'd tell us to take it easy and go to the track and bet on a few races. During the playoffs, he'd give us days off between games. He believed he'd get more out of you if you liked him than if you hated his guts.

He placed a lot of emphasis on team spirit, and was among the earliest coaches to welcome input from the players into how to run the show. Abel established myself, Howe,

I served as an alternate captain with the Red Wings from 1956-65.

Sugar Jim Henry was my goalie with Indianapolis in 1950-51, but here he's with the Boston Bruins and I'll show him no mercy. I scored on this play.

Bill Gadsby and Delvecchio as player assistant coaches during the early 1960s. We all had input on the goings-on with the team. He felt that two or three minds working together were better than just one person always seeking the solution to the problem.

The system we used in Detroit was to pair youngsters with veterans and let them learn the ropes from the more experienced guy. We used whomever was a veteran in that role. That's what Sid did for Gordie and Ted, and on defence, I started with Leo Reise as my partner. Leo Reise was a major influence, as was Bob Goldham and as was Red Kelly. You were able to learn from the veterans. We had regularly scheduled meetings. If you were on the power play, you discussed the power play. If you were on the penalty kill, you discussed the penalty kill.

I paired with Reise and then Goldham, and then Benny Woit. Reise, I loved the man. I still talk to him and his wife Geraldine. Goldy was probably the guy that helped me the most, because I only played the one year with Leo. Goldham should be in the Hall of Fame. There's no doubt. He was the best shot blocker short of Al Arbour. He played with me and I carried the puck. I had speed, so he let me rush and he covered back for me.

Goldy was tops. He went out of his way to help me over the rough spots. Sometimes today, when I am scouting a game and I see a young defenceman struggling out on the ice, I think, I guess they all can't be as lucky as I was. For five years, I played alongside Bob Goldham.

Goldy and I started the play where the defenceman went against the side boards and the other defenceman would give him the puck to get it out of the zone, the breakout play.

Bob Goldham was one of my first defence partners in Detroit. He made the game easy for a young player.

Goldy, he used my speed. He knew he could count on my speed so that I would get to the spot in time. I was out of there like a bat out of hell.

You can't talk about those Detroit glory years without spending a lot of time discussing the role of Howe, the man they so appropriately call Mr. Hockey. Howe, he was unbelievable: for and against. Gordie Howe is a remarkable fellow, on and off the ice.

I actually started the play that led to Gordie's 545th NHL goal on November 10, 1963 at the Olympia, the tally that pushed him past Rocket Richard and into top spot on the league's all-time goals list.

We were short-handed, killing off a five-minute high-sticking major to Alex Faulkner, who'd accidentally clipped Montreal's Ralph Backstrom over the left eye, opening a two-stitch cut. The Canadiens brought the puck into our end of the rink, but I won a battle in the corner and dished a short pass off to Gordie.

Howe then fed a long pass to Billy McNeill in the neutral zone, and jumped up to join him on the rush along with my defence partner Bill Gadsby. It was a three-on-two with Jacques Laperriere and Dave Balon back for Montreal

and I remember Gordie yelling, "Let's get going," as the three of them broke up ice.

Balon moved toward McNeill and Laperriere broke in Howe's direction, but McNeill hit Gordie with a perfect pass and he zipped a low hard shot into the net between the post and the left skate of Canadiens goalie Charlie Hodge.

Pandemonium ensued. Our bench emptied; Faulkner even poured out of the penalty box to congratulate Gordie. I remember that at the end of the game, Montreal's Henri Richard, the Rocket's little brother, came over and shook Gordie's hand. I thought that was a classy gesture. And I also remember another thing that puzzled me. For some reason, I wasn't credited with an assist on the record goal.

Throughout the drive to that record there was tremendous attention focused on Gordie. We tried not to mention the mark to him, but we pulled for him silently. We just let him do his own thing. We didn't put any pressure on him.

Everybody knows what Gordie did on a hockey rink. But it's what he did—and continues to do—off the ice, at home and on trips, that continues to amaze me. He's never too busy to give autographs. During his playing

82

days, when we were on the road, he'd often spend two or three hours answering mail that had accumulated at Detroit's Olympia, sending out autographed pictures. It must have cost him $300-$400 a year in stamps alone.

He was and still is a great influence on younger players. If a young fellow asked him for advice or instruction, he'd respond immediately. Later in my career, when I was playing for Toronto, one night I took a run at him. He waited for me after the game. I had said, "Look out, Gordie," before I got to him on the ice, and he thanked me for that.

That was probably because he remembered the night in Montreal in 1958 when I accidentally hit him. I guess it was one of the craziest things that ever happened to me and Gordie. There was a faceoff in our end of the rink. As usual in such situations, Gordie was taking the faceoff for us.

Just before the faceoff, I skated over and whispered to him that he was to step aside as the puck dropped. I wanted to get a reef at the player who had belted me pretty good on an earlier play, Montreal's Bert Olmstead. But the play got fouled up. Gordie shifted right into the line of fire. I missed Olmstead and hit Howe. Broke his shoulder. He was out six games.

Naturally, I felt pretty lousy about that. But all Gordie said in the first-aid room was, "Marcel, you're a rotten bodychecker. You'd better get your eyes tested."

Gordie, Terry Sawchuk and I used to challenge each other off the ice by competing to see who could complete that day's newspaper crossword puzzle the quickest. And in the spring of 1959, after Detroit missed the playoffs, both Gordie and I were hired to work as television analysts for the Stanley Cup playoffs with Hockey Night In Canada. Gordie would work the English broadcast, while I was on the French-language telecast. We'd put our heads together each night to select the three stars after the game.

It was a treat to be on a team with him. Every player that ever played with Gordie would tell you the same thing. He was something special in any sport.

Those championship teams, they were built from a solid core. Beyond the stars, we had the grinders, guys like Marty Pavelich, Bill Dineen and Metro Prystai, who did the dirty work. From the Red Wings system came players such as Dutch Reibel, Johnny Bucyk and Glenn Hall. Then there was Norm Ullman, who was a super player, but a victim of bad timing.

Toronto goalie Ed Chadwick stacks the pads to foil me after the feed from Gordie Howe.

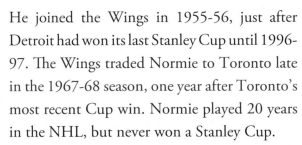

He joined the Wings in 1955-56, just after Detroit had won its last Stanley Cup until 1996-97. The Wings traded Normie to Toronto late in the 1967-68 season, one year after Toronto's most recent Cup win. Normie played 20 years in the NHL, but never won a Stanley Cup.

We'd change coaches and we'd keep winning. Tommy Ivan was my first NHL coach when I came up for the 1950 Stanley Cup playoffs. Ivan was a gentleman. You couldn't meet a nicer guy. That's why we had him up on our shoulders when we won in 1952. I'm the guy that first hoisted him up.

85

When Tommy left Detroit to take over as coach and GM in Chicago after our Cup win in 1954, Jimmy Skinner replaced him behind the bench. I originally played for Jimmy while he was coaching the Windsor Spitfires after Detroit first signed me a to C-form contract back in 1947, so we had a history together. Jimmy was a different coach than he was in junior, though. He coached me much quicker than Tommy Ivan did. Tommy left it to Leo and Bobby, the veteran defencemen, to show me the ropes. Jimmy was much more hands-on. Jimmy was a good coach, but he was helped a lot by Lindsay. Good with the kids and far from being an autocratic boss, Skinner relied heavily on his captains and other veterans. He was very much dependent on the older players on the team. He worked them as a family.

After we'd won the title again in the spring of 1955, *The Hockey News* forecasted in its 1955-56 preview issue that Detroit was plotting "to imprison the Stanley Cup for all time," even though the club had undergone a serious roster overhaul during the off season.

Our GM Jack Adams was a trader and the summer of 1955 was no different. Adams was noted for shaking up the team's chemistry over the years, and he shook it up again six weeks after the team won the championship. He traded away half of our team in two trades only five days apart. First, he sent Tony Leswick, Johnny Wilson, Glen Skov and Woit to Chicago. Shortly thereafter, Sawchuk, Vic Stasiuk, Marcel Bonin, and Lorne Davis went to Boston.

To say we were shocked would be putting it lightly. It would have been different if the team was aging, but it wasn't. It seemed as if Jack evaluated his hockey club based on personality rather than ability and he thought, having won

86

Two Hall of Fame defencemen—Red Kelly and myself—flank fellow defenceman Jim Morrison, who played for Detroit during the 1959-60 season.

so often, it was his influence that did it. But he wasn't the one putting on the skates. He definitely took the heart and character out of that team with those deals and he didn't get much in return.

By the time we reported for training camp in the fall, only nine players—Howe, Lindsay, Reibel, Delvecchio, Kelly, Dineen, Goldham, Larry Hillman and myself—were left from the team which had won the Stanley Cup only a few months before.

I have to admit, I still have a soft spot for Adams because he treated me so well. I will say this about him: he deserves credit as the person who promoted and established hockey in Detroit and Michigan. People thought he was hard to get along with, but whenever I had a problem, I'd go to his office and he'd say, "Come on in and close the door, son, and let's talk about it."

The blockbuster trading, it was nothing new to Adams, who had been manager of Detroit since 1927 and worked under the theory that championship-calibre teams have an average lifespan of five years. He had reshaped the Detroit club which played in the finals six times in the 1940s and won Stanley Cups in 1950, '52, '54 and '55.

A lot of people criticize the old man's deals then, but he made others which worked out previously, including the blockbuster deals which helped mold the 1949-50 Cup championship squad. The Pete Babando deal with Boston got us a Stanley Cup in 1950 when Babando scored the winner in Game 7 in overtime. George Gee won the faceoff on that goal and he came over in a deal with Chicago. Leswick, who scored our Cup-winning goal in 1954, joined us from New York.

This time, though, the swaps didn't meet up to expectations. Of the eight players we received in the deals, only two, Warren Godfrey and Bucky Hollingworth, were still around after the following season, and within three years, Sawchuk, Wilson and Leswick were reacquired. You can't say for sure whether we would have won more Cups, but it certainly does make you think.

Certainly, things didn't look that dire at first. Although Montreal ended our record seven-season first place run in 1955-56 and won the Stanley Cup, we did play the Canadiens in the final that spring. And the next season, 1956-57, we were right back on top of the regular-season standings again. But we were stunned by Boston in a five-game semifinal upset. In 1958-59, we missed the playoffs for the first time since the 1937-38 season. It was a good year for me, though. I finished second in the Norris Trophy voting as the NHL's best defenceman to Montreal's Doug Harvey.

The next season, there were more trades. Red Kelly was dealt to New York in 1960, but when he refused to report and threatened to retire, the deal was voided and he was shipped to Toronto a few days later. Gadsby was supposed to come to us from the Rangers in the original Kelly trade, and after the 1960-61 season we were finally able to acquire him from the Rangers for a minor-league defenceman named Les Hunt. It was a steal of a deal. Gadsby was a Hall of Famer who played 20 years in the league.

After Red left, Bill was a great help to me. We were the anchors at the back. We were really the only veteran defenders on those early 1960s Red Wings clubs. It was our job to mentor up-and-comers such as Howie Young, Pete Goegan, Gerry Odrowski and Gary Bergman, just as guys like Reise and Goldham had mentored me when I first broke into the league.

Late in the 1959-60 season, I got quite a surprise and a rare treat for an athlete. I was recognized with a night, but surprisingly, not in Detroit. I was honoured with a Marcel Pronovost night in Montreal, at the Forum prior to a March 5, 1960 game against the Canadiens. It was pretty rare for a Red Wing to get an ovation in Montreal. I was very happy, and overwhelmed by emotion. It says something about how I was viewed in other NHL cities. My friends from the Montreal suburb of Beauharnois, where I lived in the summer months, presented me with a car, and my teammates gave me the gift of a diamond ring. It was reported as the first time in NHL history that a visiting player had been honoured with such a night of recognition. It had a lot to do with me being from Quebec and having so many friends in the area. Back in Detroit, I had been dubbed "Detroit's own Flying Frenchman" by Olympia fans.

I'd make three more appearances in the Stanley Cup final with the Wings, all of them built around solid defence and a little bit of luck. In all three of those appearances, we'd finished fourth during the regular season, grabbing the last playoff position. In 1960-61, we even posted a losing record, going 25-29-16, but rose up and upset second-place Toronto in the semifinals. "Those guys just wanted to win and you couldn't stop them," Leafs assistant

My wife Cindy and I at centre ice at the Montreal Forum the night of March 5, 1960, when the Canadiens honoured me prior to our game that night.

GM King Clancy said. "You won't see three players perform any better than Gordie Howe, Terry Sawchuk and Marcel Pronovost did in this series."

We lost to Chicago in a six-game final series that spring, a set that I labored through thanks to a serious injury. We were practicing and I went to turn out of the way of a Normie Ullman shot and it hit me right in the ankle, breaking it. It wasn't that much of a weight-bearing bone, but it was serious enough that they wouldn't let me play. I missed Games 2 and 3. "You don't walk down the bench and find another Pronovost," Abel told reporters. He also informed the media that my injury was just a badly bruised right ankle, but it was broken. I was sitting in the press box at Olympia Stadium watching us win Game 2 of the series by a 3-1 score when Harold Ballard, one of the owners of the Toronto Maple Leafs, nodded toward me and said, "If they had that guy, they'd be home free."

Then they said, "Well, we need you. Would you mind being injected?" It was tender. But I said "okay." I wouldn't even take the warm-up. I would walk into the rink on crutches with a removable cast on my ankle. They'd remove the cast, then I would get all dressed for the game except for that one foot. Just five minutes before the national anthem, they would come in with the needles, inject my ankle and I would lace up my skate and go play. But because I was so active, it would wear out. You talk about the pain of a toothache, well imagine the pain I was in. What they would do is put my foot in a bucket of ice, then hot water, then a bucket of ice, then hot water. We were deadlocked 2-2 after four games, but the Black Hawks won the next two and took the series. If I'd have been healthy, we might have won another Cup.

That 1960-61 campaign was the first full season in which the Wings had played without Red Kelly on defence. I was the unquestioned number one man on Detroit defence now and the hockey experts recognized my contribution when I was named to the defence for the

NHL's First All-Star Team that season for the second campaign in succession. I think my biggest personal satisfaction was being able to play in the NHL for 21 seasons, but my biggest individual thrill was the night I'd learned I'd made the First All-Star team for the first time. And I made it both years alongside a pretty good defenceman, Montreal's Doug Harvey, who won the Norris Trophy as the NHL's best defender seven times.

Amazingly, we'd miss the playoffs again in 1961-62, but were right back in the final series again in 1962-63, this time against the Toronto Maple Leafs. Those Toronto-Detroit series were quite different from what you see today, where the fan base across the border from Detroit in Windsor is split down the middle.

The Wings would often black out *Hockey Night In Canada* broadcasts of Leafs games during that era, angering local hockey fans and turning them against the Red Wings. When I first played in Detroit, everyone in Windsor was either a Montreal or Toronto fan. It didn't really influence how we played. We were professionals. We used to joke that whenever we played the Canadiens or Toronto at the Olympia, there were more fights in the stands than on the ice. When I came back in 1980 as a Red Wings assistant coach, I was shocked to see how many Detroit fans there were in Windsor.

Toronto whipped us pretty good in 1963, taking the set in five games, but my work in defeat earned high praise. *Windsor Star* writer Matt Dennis referred to me as "the underrated player in this series. At the age of 32, he is turning in some of the best hockey of his career."

I was only 19 when I played in my first Cup final series in 1950, but this time around,

I was among the senior members of the defensive corps, so I felt qualified to offer my opinion on how the game had changed over those 13 years.

"Now there is more scoring," I told Dennis. "That is what is selling the game, as the public wants to see plenty of goals. It's a little tougher for defencemen, as we have to be able to lead a rush. If you're not a two-way rearguard, you'll find it hard to draw a following. Hockey is the fastest game, and the opportunities for

I scored 14 times on New York Rangers goalie Gump Worsley, more than any other netminder.

bodychecking are not as numerous as they used to be. Only a fast skater can make the NHL. Coaching has progressed, and even rookies come into the league now knowing that they must keep their heads up. Hockey is a team game and that means discipline and to many a youth today that reasoning is hard to understand. There must be a leader with authority, whether it be the coach or team captain. All the great hockey players that I have ever met have always shown respect to those more experienced in charge of the team."

A year later, the Cup final outcome was an entirely different story. We should have won the Cup in the spring of 1964. We held 2-1 and 3-2 leads in the series, and after beating Toronto 2-1 in Game 5 of the set at Maple Leaf Gardens, were coming back to Olympia Stadium with a chance to take the Cup on home ice in Game 6.

The legend of that game is still talked about in Stanley Cup lore. We had taken a 3-2 lead on a goal by Howe, but Billy Harris tied it for the Leafs late in the second period. After a scoreless third frame, we headed to overtime. Early in the extra frame, Toronto defenceman Bobby Baun, who was playing with a hairline ankle fracture, lofted a shot toward our goal.

It deflected off Gadsby's stick, over Sawchuk's shoulder and in for the winner at 2:43 of overtime. Baun's goal, it was like Leswick's goal that won us the Cup in 1954. Just a flukey bounce, that's all.

I bled over that one. I had a chance to get a goal that night and I missed the opportunity. I hit the post in overtime. That Game 6 loss, it took the life right out of us. Andy Bathgate scored for Toronto three minutes into Game 7, and we just gave up. The Leafs shut us out 4-0 and the Cup was theirs.

That was my eighth Stanley Cup final, and my fourth Game 7 in a final series, a Stanley Cup record I share with three other players. I'd also played in Game 7 of the 1950, 1954, and 1955 final series, winning all three times. Lindsay played in Game 7 of the 1945 final as well as 1950-54-55, also going 3-1. Howe was in Game 7 in 1954-55-63-64, and was 2-2. Likewise, longtime Montreal captain Jean Beliveau was 2-2 in Cup final Game 7s, winning in 1965 and 1971 after losing to the Wings in 1954-55.

Bathgate broke our hearts that night. But a year later, he and I would be the launching points in a blockbuster deal that would forever change my hockey landscape.

Gordie Howe's recollection of the Pronovost hit that broke his collarbone:

"While playing with Marcel, he broke my collarbone with a good, stiff bodycheck. Actually, he was aiming for Bert Olmstead and he hit me. So I knew that Marcel could hit and hit hard."

Going to Toronto was the best thing that happened to my career. My salary instantly doubled.

CROSSING THE BRIDGE
A SUPRISING MOVE ACROSS THE BORDER

I WAS DRIVING ACROSS THE AMBASSADOR BRIDGE, leaving Detroit and headed for Windsor on the afternoon of May 20, 1965, when I suddenly found out I'd be leaving Detroit for good.

I was listening to the radio when a report came over the airwaves with some shocking news. I'd just been dealt to the Toronto Maple Leafs. I couldn't believe it. It was like being rejected by your mother. I'd spent 18 years in the Detroit organization. It wasn't until much later, around 11 in the evening, when Johnny Mitchell, who was the assistant to Red Wings coach-GM Sid Abel, called my Windsor home to break the official news that I'd been traded.

The Wings sent forwards Ed Joyal, Larry Jeffrey, and Lowell MacDonald, along with defence-men Autry Erickson and me to the Leafs for forward Andy Bathgate, who had scored the Stanley Cup-winning goal for Toronto against Detroit in Game 7 of the 1964 Stanley Cup final, and for-wards Gary Jarrett and Billy Harris. It started out as a one-for-one deal—Bathgate for me—and just grew from there as Abel and Toronto coach-GM Punch Imlach kept talking. "Sid and I decided we might as well make it a jim-dandy of a trade and he gave me five for three," Imlach explained.

In the days immediately after the trade, my mind was spinning. At first, I went into shock, and then into seclusion for about a day. Old friends and teammates called to offer best wishes. It's tough to cut 18 years off your life. I was 34 and I'd been with the Detroit organization since I was 16 years old. I had hoped that there might be a position for me within the organization after my playing days were done.

My life in hockey flashed before my eyes. I thought about how I'd donned my first pair of skates at the age of four and here I was, 31 years later, still wearing skates for a living. I thought back to my time in Shawinigan and winning that provincial midget title with Jacques Plante in goal. I recalled that fateful day in the winter of 1946, when Red Wings scout Marcel Cote came to check out the Wilson brothers and discovered me at the same time. I pondered my junior days in Windsor with the Spitfires, those first-place finishes and that lost Memorial Cup. The people in Windsor were great to us. That was the team that started junior hockey booming in Windsor and it was also why we decided to make our winter home in Windsor while I played for the Wings. It also dawned on me that I was the last of those players who had reported to Windsor in the fall of 1947 to play for Jimmy Skinner's Spitfires to leave the Detroit franchise.

I also thought about my little brother Jean, who'd won the Memorial Cup in the spring of 1965 with the Niagara Falls Flyers. He was the property of the Boston Bruins back then and I figured it wouldn't be long before we'd see him skate in the NHL. I was thinking about how much I'd love to play against him, how I'd like to give him a good solid check to welcome him to the league.

While I wasn't about to say, "I quit," I still wanted to know what plans the Leafs had for me before committing to their team. I didn't really know what was going to happen, what

lay ahead for me. At my age, I wanted some security and I wanted to find out what Punch had in mind, what he expected and what the team had to offer.

When the trade was made, I'll admit it, I was hurt, but I turned around quickly. It's hard to move after being in one place for a long time, but I was well-received by Punch, and that helped a lot.

Punch described me as an "illustrious player in his own right. Pronovost will help shore up the left side of our defence, where we had trouble all last season." Abel countered by admitting the team would miss my presence along the blue line. "We've weakened our defence, but the men we got could add 60 goals to the offence," he'd reasoned.

This trade happened in the off season, but I knew that Punch was after me, because he'd talked to me in Montreal and he said, "Would you mind playing for me?" I said I can play for anybody. That was not long before the trade was made.

From what I understood, I was asked for in the trade and that makes you feel as though you can help a team. I was flattered that Punch wanted me. I looked upon it as a good omen, because he had a reputation for liking older

I won my fifth Stanley Cup on the Leafs' blue line in the spring of 1967.

of 1965, as I was attending my first training camp as a Maple Leaf, he walked out on the team and announced his retirement from hockey, right in the prime of his career. He said he was going to attend university at McMaster in Hamilton and play for the football team.

He ended up playing hockey in the International League with Muskegon and later in Finland and for the Canadian national team. Punch traded Brewer's rights to the Red Wings in 1968 and he made a comeback in the NHL with Detroit in 1969. Brewer made the NHL All-Star Team following the 1969-70 campaign. Like I said, he was a great player, but he threw away some of the best years of his career.

Even without Brewer, we were deep in defencemen on the Toronto roster. The Leafs suited up three future Hall of Famers—Tim Horton, Allan Stanley and me. After that trio, there was Bobby Baun, Kent Douglas, who'd been the NHL's rookie of the year in 1962-63, Larry Hillman and Al Arbour. I paired with Hillman for most of my time in Toronto.

I'd played with both Larry and Al in Detroit when they first came up to the NHL in the mid-1950s. Al was part of our 1953-54 Stanley Cup-winning club. Like me, he'd played his junior hockey for the Windsor Spitfires. He went from Detroit to Chicago, where he won a Stanley Cup, and he also won Stanley Cups with Toronto, but he was never able to establish himself as an NHL regular. I could never understand why Al didn't stick in the NHL. He was a tremendous shot blocker and I'd have to rate him ahead of a few guys who'd been drawing regular paycheques in this league while he struggled to make the grade for good.

Al, who was the last NHLer who played the game while wearing eyeglasses, finally got a regular job in the NHL with the St. Louis Blues following the 1967 expansion and played in three Stanley Cup finals with them. Of course, everyone remembers him as coach of the New York Islanders when they won four straight Stanley Cups from 1980-83. Al is in the Hall of Fame, too, but it's because of his coaching success.

In Toronto, a lot of players complained about Punch's long, hard practice regimen. We would practice longer and harder than any other team in the league. I remember being the first player off the ice after one of his demanding workouts and a reporter wanted to know how I was able to leave early. "You have to work the hardest to get off first," I told him.

I especially remember training camp at Peterborough, Ontario in 1968. Punch would have us up at 6:30 in the morning to view video sessions of our previous day's scrimmage. Off the ice, he instilled a military training regimen under the direction of Major W.J. MacLeod of the Canadian Forces base in Kingston, Ontario. I would have needed a crystal ball to foretell if the program would prolong my career, but I knew I felt better than I had the year before.

Punch's theory was that veteran players needed more ice time to maintain their sharpness. "It especially applies to the old guys," Punch would explain of his harsh practice schedule. "They're the ones who need the extra work the most, because when a guy gets older, it's tougher for him to keep that edge. You know what I'd like to do with my guys? I'd like to make them work from nine to five every day, with maybe an hour out for lunch. What's so tough about that?"

Imlach imposed twice-daily practices when the club wasn't playing well, the second one being just for punishment. He would call it for 3:30 in the afternoon, so by 4 o'clock, 4:30, 5 o'clock, you had showered and were right in the heavy traffic going home. That was supposed to be the price we paid, but little did

he know that the majority of the guys would adjourn to a bar nearby, have a couple of beers and then go home, so we defeated his purpose.

I guess all the hard work was designed to keep the fluids flowing through our joints so we didn't seize up from lack of use. We used to joke that if you suffered a heart attack, Punch would recommend extra skating to work out the problem. I never minded the work and Bower also thrived on it, but others expressed their distaste

Although I was at first apprehensive about coming to Toronto, joining the Leafs proved to be a wise move. I won another Stanley Cup and it led to my career in coaching.

for Punch's views. Bathgate, the key fellow who left the Leafs and went to Detroit in the trade for me, was especially vocal in his criticism of Punch's thoughts on practice habits.

"There's a limit to a player's endurance," Bathgate suggested after he was dealt to the Red Wings. "Imlach pushed a few of the players past that limit physically and mentally."

More than a demanding taskmaster, Punch was also an innovator. Punch used quite a bit of video. He was one of the first coaches to do so. Punch was a funny guy in terms of the treatment of his players. He believed in special treatment for special athletes, except for big Frank. That was Frank Mahovlich; the Big M. Punch, he'd always be on Frank's case. He couldn't play for Punch in a month of Sundays.

Frank was our best goal scorer, but he was an emotional sort. You never knew why Punch did it, why he rode Frank so hard. When Punch dished out criticism, Frank was always near the top of his list. He'd even pronounce his name incorrectly, referring to Frank as "Maholovich." Maybe the reason he did things like that was because he thought Frank had more to give and that sort of thing would push Frank's buttons. I don't know for sure, but I do know that it got to a point that during the

1967-68 season, Frank had to leave the team for a while after suffering a nervous breakdown. Frank was a guy who needed encouragement, not criticism.

Frank poured his heart out to me whenever he got down. Frank's wife Marie, she poured her heart out to me as well. I never had problems with Imlach, so maybe they thought I could reason with Punch on Frank's behalf. Marie, she used to come to me and say, "Can you speak to that son of a bitch?" And Imlach, he kind of listened to me when I talked to him about it.

One guy who seemed to be able to get Punch's ear on a regular basis was Armstrong, Toronto's long-time captain. Chief, as everybody called George because of his Native Canadian heritage, he was an ideal captain, a real leader. He was the absolute greatest captain that I've ever played with in all my years in the game. When one of the players wasn't going right, Armstrong had a way of chewing him out that wouldn't make the guy feel bad, but rather, he'd feel good about himself. George possessed a great sense of humour and he could lighten a serious mood very quickly in the dressing room.

The one thing with him was that he dominated Imlach a little bit, so if you were in the

Tangling for position with Boston's Phil Esposito while my defence partner Larry Hillman looks on. My last full NHL season was with the Leafs in 1968-69.

doghouse with Imlach, Chief could act as a go-between and kind of smooth over the waters.

Late in my first training camp as a Maple Leaf on October 17, 1965, we came to Olympia Stadium for an exhibition game against the Red Wings. As fate would have it, we whipped Detroit 3-1 and I registered a goal and an assist.

Windsor Star columnist Jack Dulmage wrote that "Pronovost looked as if he could help the Red Wings, which will be a subject under discussion for possibly the whole season, because the Detroit club has no one in sight who can do what Marcel did."

Even Abel seemed a little perplexed by this point in time as to how he was going to replace me on Detroit's back end. "Maybe we can make a deal for another defenceman," he said. "We've also got some promising young defencemen in our farm system that will be given a close look at camp."

I won't lie. It felt good to know that Detroit was missing me from the lineup. All players have pride. I prided myself on being able to do it all on the ice. I could skate, puckhandle, make plays and put it in the net when required. And I was equally adept without the puck, armed with tremendous lateral movement that made me a devastating open-ice bodychecker. I was more

of a complete defenceman. All around, I tried to excel in all aspects of the game, and I succeeded, because I played 21 years in the NHL.

Even Gordie Howe paused to comment on what I'd meant to the Red Wings over the years and what he thought of me as a player. "Marcel is a quiet individual," Gordie noted. "He doesn't brag. He does more complaining about his own play, criticizing himself. That's probably one of the things that make him such a fine hockey player."

During my time with the Wings, certainly our number-one rivals were the Montreal Canadiens. We played them four times in the Stanley Cup final between 1952-56 and there's nothing like that sort of competitive environment to ramp up a rivalry. But our feud with Toronto was a close second. It was more based in grudge matches than tradition. When he was with the Wings, Sid Abel used to say that they paid him to play the other teams. He played against the Leafs for free. That was how much he hated Toronto. It was always an intense rivalry. People always talk about Toronto-Montreal, but Toronto-Detroit was just as much of a battle.

Early into my first Maple Leafs campaign, a momentous game occurred. A 4-2 win over the New York Rangers on November 28, 1965 marked the 1,000th regular-season game of my NHL career. I was the seventh player in NHL history to reach the milestone, following three of my old Detroit teammates—Howe, Ted Lindsay and Bill Gadsby—two of my current Leafs teammates—Red Kelly and Stanley—and former Montreal defenceman Doug Harvey. Back then, it wasn't like it is today. There was barely a mention of the accomplishment. Nowadays, players are presented milestone achievements awards when they reach 1,000 games.

Midway through my first season with the Leafs, I was put on the sidelines by my first serious injury in many seasons. In a January 29, 1966 game against the New York Rangers, I suffered strained knee ligaments. I still can recall the play. Rangers forward Earl Ingarfield was coming at me and I stuck out my leg. He hit me from the outside, pushing my knee in. It cost me 16 games that season and was the start of a series of knee ailments that would plague the later years of my career.

Speaking of knee injuries, I played a role in the saga of what likely remains the most infamous run of knee injuries in NHL history. One of my stiff bodychecks was the cause of

The Stanly Cup ring I got with the Leafs in 1967.

the first of Bobby Orr's numerous knee ailments that would eventually scuttle the career of the superstar Boston Bruins defenceman in 1978 at the young age of 30.

It was during a December 4, 1966 game between the Leafs and Bruins, Orr's rookie season in the NHL. He kept coming down and going to my side. My partner on the right was Hillman, so I told him to drop off and open up the middle for him. I could skate with Orr, but I got tired of chasing him. What I did is I went up a little higher and picked him up a little earlier. What he didn't realize was that I could skate as fast backwards as he could forward. He got right in front of the Boston bench, just by the blue line and turned outside and that's when

105

I knew I had him. I hit him squarely. I caught him with my hip and just about threw him into their bench. Orr suffered injuries to the internal ligaments in his left knee and missed eight games after my punishing hit.

We had a lot of characters on those Leafs teams. Eddie Shack was known as the Entertainer and the Clown Prince of hockey. He didn't see a lot of ice time and was always in Punch's doghouse because he'd freelance so much on the ice, but we appreciated his toughness, especially his willingness to tangle

with Montreal's John Ferguson, the NHL's heavyweight champion. Before Ferguson came along, up until then, there really wasn't anything like the modern enforcer in the original six era of the league. Everyone was their own enforcer. If you weren't tough enough, you were sent to the minors. That's a place you didn't want to go because that's where the real enforcers played in those days.

We had tried to get Shack to Detroit from New York in the Red Kelly trade, but when Red refused to report to New York, the Leafs

106

Toronto captain George Armstrong and I come back to help Terry Sawchuk defend against Montreal's Roadrunner, the speedy and pesky Yvan Cournoyer.

managed to not only get Kelly out of Detroit, they later acquired Shack from the Rangers. Shackie was so popular in Toronto, they wrote a song about him—Clear The Track, Here Comes Shack—and someone even named a racehorse after him.

Much was made about Eddie's lack of formal education. He didn't really learn to read until he joined the Leafs and Imlach helped him take classes at De La Salle high school in Toronto. One night when the Leafs were playing Detroit at Maple Leaf Gardens, old man Adams was riding Eddie hard, scolding him by suggesting that not only couldn't Eddie get a goal, he couldn't even spell the word. Well, don't you know it, Eddie put the puck in the net, then skated quickly over to the Detroit bench, throwing up snow as he came to a sudden stop. Then he stood there and spelled out S-C-O-R-E.

Another guy we saw briefly in Toronto during my early time with the Leafs was goaltender Gary Smith. Like my brother Claude, Gary was a well-travelled netminder who shared the nickname Suitcase. Smith also stood six-foot-four, which today is commonplace among goalies, but back in those days, was rarely seen. Smith also possessed a strange notion that he

was going to be the first NHL puckstopper to score a goal. He'd actually scored a goal in 1962 while playing junior, so there was precedence behind his thinking.

When both Bower and Sawchuk were hurt, Smith was called up from the minor leagues and got into a game in which we were losing very badly at the Montreal Forum. Well, the next thing you know, he's got the puck and he's skating up the ice, stickhandling his way past the blue line toward the centre red line. About three feet from centre, Smith tried to take a shot and flubbed it. Montreal defenceman J.C. Tremblay corralled the puck and fired it toward our vacated net, where I found myself playing some impromptu goal and made a kick save on the long shot.

When I arrived in Toronto, the Leafs had just been dethroned as Stanley Cup champions, replaced by the Canadiens in the spring of 1965. Montreal also bounced us quickly from the playoffs the following year, sweeping the Leafs aside in a rapid four-game semifinal series.

The experts were saying that the Leafs were done, that Punch's old guard was worn out and had nothing left to give. They were writing us off, but we were about to write a remarkable final chapter.

107

Gary Smith's recollection of Pronovost's big save against Montreal:

"It was my first NHL game. This was in the old six-team NHL and I didn't know if I'd ever play another game. They scored three or four goals and I thought, 'I'm going to get the hook. What can I do to make people remember that I played in the NHL?' So I thought I would go down the ice and try to score.

"I came up to centre ice with the puck. Montreal defenceman J.C. Tremblay didn't know what to do. He never hit a guy in his life, but then he decided to take a run at me. He nailed me. I was at the red line and I was spinning around. I saw Punch Imlach pull his hat down over his head on the first spin, and on the second spin I saw Marcel Pronovost make a great save on Tremblay's long shot."

Windsor Spitfires defencemen who also played for the Toronto Maple Leafs:

Larry Hillman (1960-68)

Marcel Pronovost (1965-70)

Al Arbour (1961-66)

Joel Quenneville (1978-80)

Darwin McCutcheon (1981-82)

Craig Muni (1981-86)

Todd Gill (1984-96)

Chris Kotsopoulos (1985-89)

Darryl Shannon (1988-93)

D. J. Smith (1996-2000)

Dave Keon is about to fill the Stanley Cup with champagne and I'm all smiles as I wait for a sip of bubbly.

WON FOR THE AGED
A KEY COG IN TORONTO'S LAST STANLEY CUP TRIUMPH

OUR COACH, PUNCH IMLACH, referred to the 1966-67 Toronto Maple Leafs as the Old Fellows Athletic Club. Comedian Johnny Wayne of Wayne & Shuster used to say about those Leafs, "It won't be knee ligament operations that do in this team. It will be prostate surgery."

Nobody gave us a chance to win that year. We were too old, too broken-down. Our best days were behind us. The Leafs had gone out of the playoffs in the first round the last two springs and most of the pre-season prognosticators weren't even giving us that chance this time around. They had us pegged for a fifth-place finish and out of the playoff picture.

Naturally, we had other ideas. The roster of that 1967 Maple Leafs club consisted of a group of players that played a traditional, if unspectacular, brand of hockey. We had less firepower than most of the teams in the league, but we knew that they couldn't beat us in two areas—work ethic and defensive play.

When you look at defensive hockey, the teams that play well behind their own blue line usually having the best chance to win. We had people who prided themselves in not giving up a goal, not coughing up the puck in their zone.

Most of the clubs today aren't as disciplined as we were. The players are all over the ice. Then they try to change and play in the playoffs like we played all during the regular season. In the spring of 1967, our Leafs team displayed to the hockey world how forwards and defencemen, when supported by clutch netminding, could implement a system that made it difficult for the opposing team to get enough goals to win.

Not that it was easy, mind you. Our two ancient warriors between the pipes, Terry Sawchuk and Johnny Bower, both endured their share of injuries and we ended up going with five different goalies that season, as Bruce Gamble and the Smiths, Al and Gary, all saw duty between the pipes. I played a role in one of the mishaps, accidentally colliding with Bower, who suffered strained back muscles.

My friend Sawchuk passed a milestone late in the season when he blanked the Chicago Black Hawks 3-0 at Maple Leaf Gardens for his 100th regular-season NHL shutout. I was the first to reach Sawchuk as the team mobbed him following his 22-save performance. He's the greatest goalie I've ever seen and among the greatest competitors. It wouldn't be the last time Terry would haunt Chicago that season.

We endured some epic struggles during the regular season and for a time it looked as if the experts might have been right. As late as mid-February, we were scrambling, out of a play-off spot, having just endured a 10-game losing streak, which was a Maple Leafs' club record for futility. To make matters worse, Imlach was hospitalized suffering from exhaustion, and his assistant King Clancy came in to take over behind the bench. Punch was even talking about permanently giving up one of his roles, either as coach or general manager. He'd done both for the team since 1958.

What's that old saying? It's always darkest before the dawn? Well, we turned the bloody thing around. We got on a roll under King and went 8-2-2, securing our playoff spot, clinching it March 19 via a 6-5 win over Detroit. We rallied from a 4-1 deficit to beat the Red Wings and I scored the fourth Toronto goal to tie things up.

Regardless, people weren't exactly ready to give us a chance of contending for the Stanley Cup. We'd drawn the first-place Black Hawks in the opening round of the playoffs. We'd finished in third place at 32-27-11 for 75 points, 19 fewer than the Black Hawks, who were loaded for bear. They'd scored the most goals in the league and allowed the fewest. Bobby Hull led the league with 52 goals and Stan Mikita was the scoring champion with an NHL-record 97 points. So deep was Chicago's talent that Punch decided it was pointless to try and shadow Hull. "It's no use," he reasoned. "They have too many good goal scorers."

On our side, Ron Ellis led us with 22 goals and Dave Keon was our top point-producer with 52. In seven regular-season games at Chicago Stadium, the Leafs had gone 0-6-1, had been outscored 26-9 and were shutout twice. The experts once more felt that the Leafs were doomed as we readied to face Chicago.

Punch, though, offered a different viewpoint. "We'll beat Chicago," he boasted to reporters on the eve of Game 1. "The fact we haven't won a game there all season must be in our favour."

Punch outlined his strategy to stunt Chicago's attack. "We've got to check them as a team," he told us. "We've got to hem them in their end, forecheck them and not allow them to start their pattern plays."

Our game plan was to keep Hull and Mikita on their backhands so that they couldn't slap the puck with their newfangled curved sticks. The other part of the plan was to punish them at every opportunity with good stiff bodychecks. We had a motto. We'd say, "Let's knock the Hawks." We played them very, very physical. It's the secret of the game. They can't score if they're on their cans. We kicked the hell out of Chicago.

Not much of it worked in Game 1. We were whipped 5-2 by the Black Hawks in the series opener at Chicago Stadium. With two days off before Game 2, Punch took us back to Toronto to practice. "I couldn't take the chance of letting my boys loose in Chicago for

He shoots...

— Jac Holland, Telegram

...and scores!

Phil Esposito scored a lot of goals in the NHL, but on this occasion, I made certain that the only thing going in the net was him. Toronto goalie Johnny Bower got out of the way just in time.

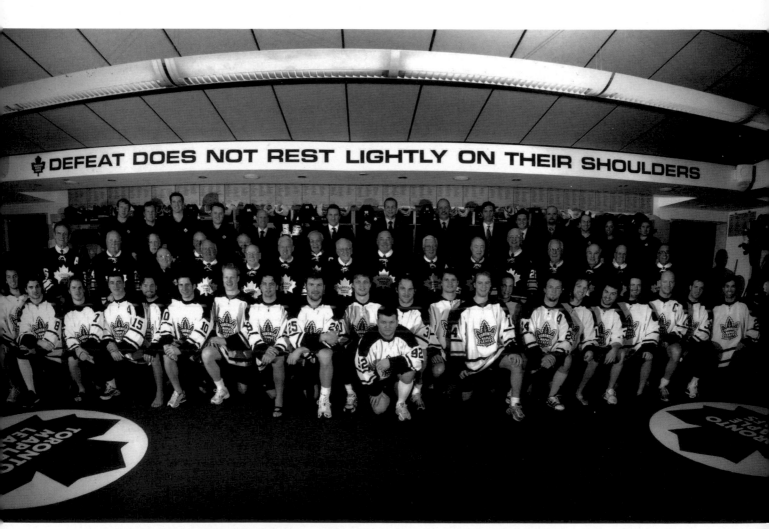

The 1967 Leafs met the current edition at our 2007 reunion. I'm right in the middle, between captain George Armstrong and Senator Frank Mahovlich.

three days," he explained. "I'd never find them when it was time to play."

Taunted by the Chicago fans after Game 1, Sawchuk made them pay in Game 2. He blocked 33 shots and we made first-period goals by Pete Stemkowski and Keon stand up for a 3-1 triumph to tie the set. But there was bad news, too. We lost our captain George Armstrong to a knee injury.

It was all Sawchuk again in Game 3. He made 35 saves, 27 of them in the first two periods, allowing us to assemble a 3-0 lead on goals by Ellis, Frank Mahovlich and Jim Pappin. We recorded another 3-1 victory to go ahead 2-1 in the series.

Chicago coach Billy Reay acknowledged the difference in the series. "Toronto is getting goaltending again," Reay said. "They suffered when Bower and Sawchuk were both out with injuries. They played a lot of tie games in the first half, but that's because they were getting that good goalkeeping."

When that Toronto team worked together, it was hard to beat. We had the same thing on that club that we'd had in our Cup-winning seasons in Detroit in the 1950s. We had balanced scoring. Every line could score. There was somebody to put the puck in the net and somebody to keep it out on every line. Tim Horton, Allan Stanley and I were all experienced defencemen, and that's another reason why we won. And we were so strong in goal. With Bower and Sawchuk, between the two of them, you couldn't get any better.

Chicago pulled even with us again, winning Game 4 by a 4-3 count, and we were headed back to Chicago Stadium deadlocked at 2-2. It was funny. No matter how well we played in our wins, our losses would start the second-guessers up again. Even when we'd win, no one gave us any credit. "Each game we beat Chicago, everybody said, "Well that's it. Chicago will turn it around now."

Bower had missed the start of the series after splitting open one of his fingers, but Imlach opted to turn to him for Game 5. But Johnny's finger still wasn't right and Sawchuk came in to start the second period with the score tied 2-2. Right from the faceoff, Hull got loose down the wing and fired one of his wicked slapshots. It hit Terry in the shoulder, glanced off his head and ricocheted into the seats behind the net. Sawchuk went down as if he'd been shot.

Amazingly, he got up and boarded up his net. Old Ukey blocked 37 shots—15 in the second period, another 22 in the third—and

115

Playing for Punch Imlach in Toronto was a rewarding experience.

all apply. He was so sensational maybe there just weren't words for it. Sawchuk described it as "My greatest thrill. Absolutely my greatest."

We were going back to Maple Leaf Gardens with a chance to close out Chicago and we didn't disappoint, posting our third 3-1 victory of the series. Sawchuk gave us another stellar effort, a 34-save performance. Rookie Brian Conacher, who'd come into the lineup when Armstrong was hurt, scored twice playing on a line with Keon and Mahovlich.

That was another key reason why we won that spring. We had a different hero every night. If you go through those two playoff series game by game, at some point you can find a moment where every player on the team made a key play. Everybody stood out at different times.

We held the Hawks to 14 goals over the six games. Mikita had just two goals. Hull chipped in four. The Hawks scored only a single goal in three of the games. In my mind, beating Chicago, that was the bigger upset. But everyone remembers Montreal in the next round. Before the playoffs, Punch had told us, "Just beat Chicago. Montreal will be easy."

We knew we had enough to beat the Canadiens. The Leafs donned new uniforms for

third-period goals by Stemkowski and Pappin gave us a 4-2 win.

A big part of our success in that game was that we killed off 10 minor penalties, but the huge factor, of course, was the goaltending. Sawchuk was fantastic. Any adjective you'd want to use to describe his performance that night—wonderful, great, unbelievable—they'd the playoffs that year, featuring a logo which was similar to the Maple Leaf on the Canadian flag to help celebrate Canada's centennial. That was also the year that Expo was held in Montreal. It opened just prior to the start of the final series and someone in Montreal's organization mentioned how nice the Stanley Cup looked in Expo 67's Quebec Pavillion, where the 1966 champion Habs had it on display. When we heard that, we decided to get it for the Ontario Pavillion.

We understood that we couldn't match the top two clubs, Chicago and Montreal, in shootouts. We knew the only way we could win, was to win the one-goal games. It was proven in the playoffs that year. We'd lose a game 6-2, but all the games we won were the close games. We excelled at that style. There was pride involved. You could make one goal go a long way.

Right before the final series started, Punch decided to stir the pot, labeling Montreal rookie Rogatien Vachon a "Junior B goalie" and insisting there was no way a Junior B goalie could beat his team. It looked like he'd eat his words after Henri Richard scored a hat-trick, chasing Sawchuk to the bench as Montreal hammered us 6-2 in Game 1.

Punch was always doing stuff and saying things like that. He wasn't one for playing it safe. I remember one game in Boston, where we used to get pushed around a bit, Imlach started Stemkowski, Tim Horton and Larry Hillman at forward, with Duane Rupp and I on defence because he wanted us to be more physical.

That was Imlach, though. I think the reason why he liked to stoke the fires, it was because he had so much faith in us as players. He was hard on us at times, but he respected his players, especially the veterans. We used to hide and try to get out of practice at times, but he wasn't that tough on the veterans. He knew he could trust you. He had faith in us. And as veterans, we knew we could trust each other. I was one of those veterans. He counted on me for everything. On the points, Hillman played the power play, Red Kelly played the power play, Horton played the power play. I killed penalties.

Punch played a hunch in Game 2. Right before the game, he told Bower he was starting in goal, and Johnny delivered the goods, blocking 31 shots for a 3-0 shutout victory. Stemkowski got the winner and Mike Walton and Horton also scored. "When you have two good goaltenders, you're not taking much of a chance," Imlach explained, and we felt the same way as players. Between Sawchuk and Bower, it didn't matter to us who was in net. We had complete faith in both of them.

The papers reported that Bower was 42 going on 50. He claimed he was 46. Nobody knew for sure what his real age was. Would you believe him? Even when he was young, he looked old.

Bower was Johnny-on-the-spot-again in Game 3. He made 60 saves on the night, 19 of them in the opening period, and we won 3-2 on Bob Pulford's goal in double overtime. That was the thing about us old war horses. We're better in a longer race. Punch felt his harsh practice regimen had paid dividends. "We trained all year for this," he said.

Pulford is one of those guys from that 1967 Leafs who doesn't get nearly enough credit for his contribution to the Cup win. Playing on our third line with youngsters Stemkowski and Pappin, he was a calming influence. He was instrumental in Toronto winning the Stanley Cup. He carried the youth line with his experience and settled them down. That trio—Pappin (7-8-15), Stemkowski (5-7-12) and Pulford (1-10-11)—were our top three scorers in the playoffs. Keon and Mahovlich were our goal scorers, but the strength of our team was that third line of Pulford, Stemkowski and Pappin.

Just as quickly, however, things turned sour for us again. Bower pulled a hamstring in the warm-up for Game 4. Sawchuk came in and struggled and we lost 6-2. Montreal coach Toe Blake viewed Bower's injury as an omen. "He'd been murder on us," Blake said. Again, people started to say the Leafs were done. But we knew differently.

We played our best hockey in the biggest games. Pride came in. We kind of mixed and matched and we played four defencemen. There wasn't any line matching with just four defencemen playing. Everybody had a certain edge. Timmy and I, Sam—that's what we called Stanley—and Timmy, Larry and I. You could play against anybody.

On the train en route to Montreal for Game 5, you would have thought we were headed for a frat party, not our biggest game of the season. I remember the guys laughing and joking like a junior team on the way to Montreal. I mentioned it to our captain George Armstrong and the Chief, of course, had a good line. He said that I shouldn't be surprised because, "Most junior teams were smarter than this bunch of yahoos."

118

That was Armstrong's style, one of the facets that made him such a great leader. He kept things loose with a never-ending barrage of quips and needles. On the ice, he showed the way with his no-nonsense, hard-work approach.

Following Montreal's win in Game 4, Punch posted photos of the Canadiens celebrating their goals in the Leafs dressing room. "A picture is worth 1,000 words," he explained.

When we lost the fourth one at home, everybody said we were finished. We'd go to Montreal, get beat and then come home and it would be all over. We had a lot of veteran players on that team, so leadership was never an issue. Mahovlich, who'd had a great series against Chicago with eight points, was one who never said very much and was always the last guy on the ice. He stood up in the dressing room before Game 5 and said, "We're going to

Judging from the faces, things aren't going well for the Leafs. Tim Horton and I wear glum expressions, while Kent Douglas definitely got carried away with the eye black. And based on the sunglasses, Terry Sawchuk must have really been having a rough go of it.

win this one, boys and then we're going home to win the Cup," and then he led the charge out onto the ice.

In Game 5, we stayed with Sawchuk in goal and he excelled under a 38-shot barrage. One of the best breakaway goalies in hockey history, Ukey absolutely stoned Ralph Backstrom on a breakaway chance moments into the game. Backstrom had scored twice for Montreal in Game 4. After Leon Rochefort gave the Canadiens a first-period advantage, Pappin tied it on a power play, then Conacher gave us the lead.

Now, it was my turn to take centre stage. With Kelly in the penalty box for interference late in the second period, Montreal defence-man J.C. Tremblay passed the puck directly onto my stick and I turned it on, heading up ice under a full head of steam. Bobby Rousseau and Yvan Cournoyer got tangled up on the boards and I broke in with Ellis on a two-on-one.

I skated over the Montreal blue line and stepped into a slapshot that zipped past Vachon on his glove side. I didn't pick any corner. All I did was close my eyes and shoot. There was no way I was going to pick my spot with a slapshot from 30 or 35 feet. Some guys could;

I couldn't. Keon clinched it with another goal and we were 4-1 winners.

My goal was a short-handed goal. It broke their backs, and it was meant to. It also paved the way for people to take notice of how solid Hillman and I had been as a defence pairing during the playoffs. We'd only been on the ice for five goals against during the entire post-season run, just one of those tallies coming while we were at even strength.

Sports Illustrated's Pete Axthelm cited me as the best defenceman in the series and Larry, he had a helluva series, too. Hillman and I, we adjusted to one another. Me being the veteran, I took most of the load. He was not a hitter. He was more of a stickhandler. He also played the power play. That left me out of it to kill the penalties. I paired with Sam and Horton at times on the penalty kill.

We knew we had to win Game 6 at Maple Leaf Gardens to capture the Cup. We wanted nothing to do with a seventh game in Montreal.

Leading up to the game, all the talk was about Sawchuk's turnaround. After the Game 4 loss, he'd received a telegram from some fellow in Newfoundland. All it read was,

120

"How much did they pay you?" Terry was deeply hurt by this, but it seemed to fire him up at the same time.

On game day, you couldn't talk to Sawchuk. I advised the other guys to just leave him alone. It was best, because he was a loner. Some of them would wonder where his mind was, but I knew that Terry would be ready when we needed him. Horton said, "Goaltending is like pitching. If Sawchuk is Sandy Koufax tonight, we win. If he isn't, as they say in Montreal, "c'est la guerre."

Leafs defenceman Bobby Baun couldn't get over the difference in Sawchuk when he was on his game. "When Ukey charges out, all you see to shoot at is a damn big goalie," Baun said.

Punch was his usual boastful self in the lead-up to the game. "We'll win it here," he guaranteed. "We don't even have transportation booked for a return trip to Montreal. We haven't even tried."

In the dressing room before the game, the atmosphere was anything but bravado. King Clancy came into the room and looked up toward the sign on the wall which said "The price of success is hard work." Then he hollered, "You see that sign fellows. That's what got you where you are tonight. If you comply

with it again tonight, it will carry you through to the Stanley Cup. I know you can do it."

On a table in the middle of the room, Punch had someone spread out $10,000 in cash, which was the bonus money we'd each get for winning the Cup. But when it came time for our pre-game talk, Imlach got all choked up. "Some of you have been with me for nine years," he said. "It has been said that I stuck with the old men so long we couldn't possibly win the Stanley Cup. For some of you it's a farewell. Go out there and put that puck down their throats."

Montreal stormed our end from the drop of the puck in Game 6, but they met a stonewall wearing No. 30 in the Leafs' net. Sawchuk refused to budge. He stopped 17 shots in a scoreless first period. Ellis gave us the lead in the second then Pappin got what would prove to be the Cup-winner when Stemkowski's pass bounced into the net off his backside. Dick Duff finally got one for Montreal, the only one of 41 pucks to get past Sawchuk.

The clock was winding down. The Canadiens pulled goalie Gump Worsley and Imlach sent a bunch of his old guard—Stanley, Horton, Armstrong, and Kelly—out to defend our one-goal lead along with Sawchuk and

121

Pulford. We all looked at each other on the bench and wondered how did Pulford get out there with all those old guys? After all, he was only 31.

We won the draw and Armstrong slid one into the empty net. The Cup was ours by a 3-1 verdict. In the room afterward, the Cup was there, the champagne was uncorked, but most of us were too pooped to party. "We only played 97 games this season," Keon said. "But it seems like a thousand."

Keon won the Conn Smythe Trophy as MVP of the playoffs and it was a good choice. Pound for pound in those playoff series, Davey was as good for us as Gordie Howe was for the Red Wings. Keon, he could skate, he could play defensively, he could score goals. Keon couldn't do it all, though. He was no hitter, so he depended on me for that.

Much is made about the age of that team. The fable of the old-time Leafs seems to grow more legendary each season and I understand, because it makes for good reading. In truth, we did have some long-in-the-tooth types. Bower was 42. Stanley was 41. Kelly was 39. Sawchuk, Horton and I were all 37 and Armstrong was 36.

Most of our age was on defence and in goal. The veterans on defence, as a unit, provided

the steadiness. Experience means a lot, but up front, after Kelly and Armstrong, we had Keon, Walton, Ellis, Conacher and Stemkowski. Pappin had a hell of a series against Chicago. Who were the old guys? There was a lot of young talent on that team as well that people tend to overlook. And they all did their share. My view is that we were an older team that had a lot of good youngsters. We were a success because of our mixture of experience, youth and our devotion to discipline and strategy. Our penalty killing was a huge part of it, but the big factor, of course, was goaltending.

Canadiens coach Toe Blake called it, "the toughest series I ever lost," and really, that was the end of the Montreal-Toronto rivalry in terms of being the two strongest dynasties in the league. Between 1944-67 Montreal (10) and Toronto (9) won 19 Stanley Cups. One of either Montreal or Toronto played in the Stanley Cup final in 22 of 24 seasons between 1943-44 and 1968-69. They met each other in the finals five times, including that 1967 Leafs triumph in Canada's Centennial Year. Our win in 1967 prevented Montreal from matching its own NHL record of five straight Cup wins. The Habs had won in 1965 and '66 and won again in 1968 and '69. The Leafs haven't even played in a Cup final since that 1967 win, and Montreal's been absent from the final since 1993. Neither team can be considered an NHL power anymore. In terms of the rivalry, I think the fans are the only ones who keep it alive now.

After the playoffs were over, it was pointed out that all four of our post-season losses had come on Thursdays and we'd lost those games by a combined score of 21-9. We became known as the never-on-Thursday team, so it was a good thing we won Game 6, because Game 7 in Montreal was scheduled for Thursday, May 4, 1967. "I don't think I'll even show up at the office on Thursday," Imlach joked.

The day after our win, the euphoria remained as we all gathered at Maple Leaf Gardens. Imlach was having a rough go of it. He felt sick from too much champagne the night before. I told him to go to the Gardens'

Posing with Larry Hillman at the reunion of the 1966-67 Leafs. As defence partners that spring, we allowed just one even-strength goal the entire playoffs.

Hot Stove Lounge and get some honey. Off he went and doesn't he come back with a full cup of honey. Then he told us all to get on the ice. "We start off for next year right now," Imlach bellowed. "Let's get going." I looked at Punch, smiled and said, "Come on boss, take it easy."

Another interesting facet about that team—four of our players had all won the Cup with Detroit in 1954-55, which at that point had been the last Stanley Cup earned by the Red Wings. It's quite a trivia question and we all got there through different routes. Kelly was the first to arrive, via a 1960 trade for Marc Reaume. Hillman, who played with 15 teams in a 22-season pro career, moved from Detroit to Chicago to Boston prior to arriving in Toronto later in 1960. Sawchuk was claimed by Toronto in the 1964 NHL intra-league draft.

I was part of a six-player trade with the Wings in 1965 and two of the other players Toronto got in that deal also played a role in our 1967 triumph. Forward Larry Jeffrey was doing solid work in the Chicago series until his season was ended by torn ligaments in his right knee. One of the players called up from the minors to help fill in for our injured players was Aut Erickson, who was also part of the deal that brought me to the Leafs. He saw his only action in Game 1 of the final series, but it was enough to get his name on the Cup.

When the playoffs were over, I'd appeared in 134 career Stanley Cup games. Only Kelly (164) and my old Detroit teammate Gordie Howe (150) had played more in the history of hockey. I didn't realize it at the time, but I'd played my last post-season game as an NHLer.

Likewise, the Leafs haven't won the Stanley Cup since the magical spring of 1967. Sure, it bothers me they haven't won it in so long. But Detroit went a long time without winning, too, from 1955 right up until 1997. Who says the Leafs won't get going and win three in the next 10 years?

It's a great hockey city. Another Cup would make the fans respect the tradition even more. The people in Toronto are starved for tradition.

124

1966-67 Stanley Cup Champion Toronto Maple Leafs

Forwards	Age				
George Armstrong	36	Bob Pulford	31	Marcel Pronovost	36
Brian Conacher	25	Eddie Shack	30	Allan Stanley	41
Ron Ellis	22	Pete Stemkowski	23		
Larry Jeffrey	26	Mike Walton	22	**Goal**	**Age**
Red Kelly	39			Johnny Bower	42
Dave Keon	27	**Defence**	**Age**	Terry Sawchuk	37
Frank Mahovlich	29	Bob Baun	30	Al Smith	21
Milan Marcetta	30	Aut Erickson	29		
Jim Pappin	27	Larry Hillman	30	**Coach-GM:** Punch Imlach	
		Tim Horton	37	**Asst. coach-GM:** King Clancy	

Terry Sawchuk gloves a loose puck, but I've got my stick cocked for a swing at it should the biscuit come loose.

TERRY AND ME
MY LONGTIME FRIENDSHIP WITH THE ENIGMATIC TERRY SAWCHUK

THE FIRST TIME I MET TERRY SAWCHUK there was no indication of the enduring friendship that would develop between the two of us. He was aloof and distant when we first talked at the Windsor Spitfires' training camp in the fall of 1947, the way he usually seemed to treat strangers. I was just another junior player and he was going to be our goaltender.

Over the years, as we played as teammates with the Detroit Red Wings and Toronto Maple Leafs, we would grow to become the closest of friends. In my opinion, Sawchuk is the greatest goaltender who ever played the game, but Terry was also a paradoxical man. He could be as surly as they come, but he was also capable of immense kindness.

When I first started with the Detroit organization, the Wings always had two training camps—one out west and one in the east. The one in the east that fall was in Kitchener-Waterloo in the old Waterloo Arena. We then met in Detroit at the common camp and that's when we found out that instead of going to Galt, we would be playing in Windsor. Sawchuk played in Galt the year before, so that's how he came to Windsor. He played four games for the Spitfires. Needless to say, we were 4-0. Then Harvey Jessiman, the goalie with Detroit's USHL farm club in Omaha, got hurt. He scratched an eyeball or something and they turned Terry pro and sent him to Omaha.

This was the start of Terry as a 17-year-old being associated with older guys. In Omaha, you had some older guys and you had some younger guys. Now, whether under the right influence or not, that's when Terry started to have a couple of beers. All the years I played in junior hockey, it was a milkshake league. He may have started going out with the older players and that's where his drinking may have begun.

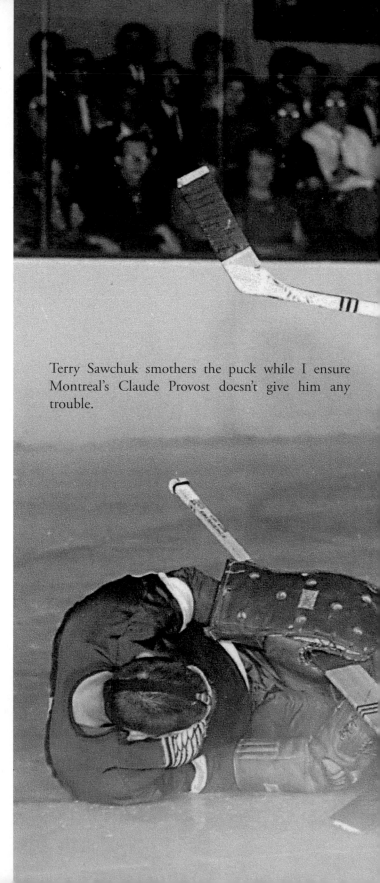

Terry Sawchuk smothers the puck while I ensure Montreal's Claude Provost doesn't give him any trouble.

The first year in Omaha, he won everything there and was named USHL rookie of the year. The next year, he ended up in the AHL with Indianapolis. Terry won all the honours again that year in Indianapolis, including the Dudley (Red) Garrett Memorial Trophy as the AHL's rookie of the year. The second year that he played there, they became the first American League club to win the Calder Cup in eight straight games. Then in 1952, he repeated the same thing in Detroit. That's when I got to know Terry, because we lived together at old lady Tannahill's boarding house on Wreford Street in Detroit. We each had a room upstairs. We each had a bedroom. But back then, he went his way and I went my way, because my crowd was different from Terry's crowd at that time.

Then I got married and we moved into an apartment building kitty-corner from the Olympia. When Terry got married to Pat in 1953, he moved into the same apartment building. It was run by Ma and Pa Russell, and besides us, Tony Leswick, Lefty Wilson, Alex Delvecchio and Ted Lindsay all had apartments in there at one time or another. Terry eventually moved out to Pontiac and got a house in Union Lake, Michigan. The fall of 1953, that's when my wife Cindy first met Pat. She and my

128

Terry Sawchuk smothers the puck while I ensure Montreal's Claude Provost doesn't give him any trouble.

Terry Sawchuk follows the puck intently while I move in along with defence partner Warren Godfrey, seeking to hold Toronto's Dave Keon and Bob Pulford at bay.

wife were both the same type of people. Very pretty, very down-to-earth. After we both got married, our wives used to get together quite a bit and we used to get together on our own.

On the ice, between the posts, that's when Terry was in his element. Without a doubt he's the greatest goaltender that I played with or against. I have a lot of respect for Glenn Hall. He was a great goalie. Jacques Plante I played with when I was 13 years old and he was another great one. Johnny Bower was a self-made goaltender. You have to give him a lot of credit. But I've always said—even when Terry was alive—that he was the greatest of them all, and I still maintain that. I don't think there are any goaltenders today that could do the job that those guys did game in and game out. They had the toughest job in sports.

Terry was determined to make it and he wasdedicated to his position. He wouldn't even go to the movies, fearful that watching the films on the big screen might put unnecessary wear and tear on his No. 1 asset as a netminder, his eyesight. He'd become a goalie at the age of 10 by inheriting the pads of his older brother Mitch, who died of a heart attack at 14. Terry talked about that and told me they were very close and that was why he became a goaltender.

Away from the rink, things didn't come so smoothly to Terry. It wasn't that he didn't like people. He just wouldn't associate with them. We all have some hang ups. He had them, I have them. In Terry's case, he had a problem demonstrating affection. For Terry to demonstrate affection was to lower his standard as a man. It was part of what made him so standoffish with people he didn't know. I think it goes back to the way he was brought up by his family. They all played a role in the end product.

I don't think Terry ever felt that he belonged anywhere. I don't think that he felt that he belonged with his family and his brothers and sisters. I think he felt that his family exploited him. And he did so much for his family, I think when it came to his own family, with his children, he wasn't going to spoil them. He had control over that and Terry was a bit of a control freak.

This is why when it came to newspapermen and other situations where he'd lose control, he'd get very aggressive. That's what made him react the way he did.

Terry always had a little bit of paranoia as far as newspapermen were concerned. He treated them very roughly, because he didn't know how to react to them. When he was on a rampage, they learned to leave him alone. Like mostly all of us, we didn't react to that pat on the back very well. We kind of stuck to our own little circle. We didn't have too many friends outside of hockey.

When he went out, Terry was looking for people that were also at the same level of notoriety as he was, so he didn't have to worry about trusting them. He could feel comfortable. That was one of the reasons he'd socialize away from the rink so often with players from the NFL's Detroit Lions.

In 1949-50, Terry garnered his first taste of NHL play, going 4-3 with a shutout and a 2.29 GAA filling in for injured Red Wings goalie Harry Lumley. Like Terry, I'd get my first NHL taste during that 1949-50 campaign, but mine would come under much more

131

pressure-packed circumstances, in the Stanley Cup playoffs, helping the Red Wings win their first Stanley Cup since the spring of 1943.

I started the next season with the Wings, and so did Terry. Detroit GM Jack Adams opted to deal Lumley away, even though he'd just backstopped the team to the Cup. That tells you the kind of confidence the Detroit organization had in Terry's ability. And it paid off. He led the NHL with 44 wins and 11 shutouts, and won the Calder Memorial Trophy as the best rookie in the league.

It was a great start, but the best was yet to come from the man we all called Ukey because of his Ukrainian heritage. During the 1951-52 season, Terry led the NHL in wins (44), shutouts (a club-record 12) and GAA (1.90) as Detroit again finished first. Then in the playoffs, he turned in a Stanley Cup performance for the ages. Terry posted shutouts in all four games played that spring at Olympia Stadium, allowing less than a goal per game (0.63) as we went 8-0 to win the Cup. It's difficult to lose when your goaltending is so good that all you need to do to win is score one goal.

The Wings won two more Cups by 1955 with Terry in goal. He's the only goalie in NHL history to post at least 30 wins and a goals-against average below two in each of his first five full seasons. But as his career progressed, the away-from-the-ice side of Terry's personality began to emerge more prominently.

Terry could be very moody, even nasty at times. I think that Terry just didn't know how to politely tell people that he wanted to be left alone, so he'd be a smartass. He didn't like the limelight and his method to avoid the spotlight was to be rude to people. It was a defence mechanism. He didn't take well to criticism or praise. I think the best word to describe him is "grumpy." But I liked him. The guys who knew Terry the best didn't take him seriously. I used to give him heck. I'd say, "Relax, take it easy. Smile." He didn't smile very often, but I got him smiling a few times.

There was a guy in Detroit who sat up near the organ loft at Olympia Stadium. That was the end of the rink where we started defending as the game got underway, so we'd be in that end for two of the three periods. And as soon as the game started, this guy would start yelling, "Hey, Sawbuck," and Terry would get pissed off. He'd say, 'Marc, can you spot that idiot?' I said, "I'm going to try." I saw the guy stand up and yell, "Hey Sawbuck," and I told Terry, "Hey, I know who it is. He's below the organ loft and to the left." This one night, Terry wasn't playing. He went up there, got behind the guy and tapped him on the shoulder. And Terry says, "I'm Sawchuk, not Sawbuck, you jackass," and then he glared at the guy. The guy was terrified, and that was the end of it. He never heckled Terry again. But the guy had got to him. It clearly had bothered Terry.

As a young player, Terry was a big kid. He was big-boned and had big shoulders. He was a pretty big guy. To play every night, he had to be in pretty good shape. His rookie year he was 219 pounds. He dropped his weight a little bit after that, but for the first three or four years that he was in Detroit, he was 207-208 during the season and maybe 210-215 in the off season. By today's standards, Terry would have probably been 14-15 percent body fat. It's still not that bad. Think about what Gump Worsley would have been on that scale.

The one thing that always stood out about Terry in those early seasons with Detroit was

Terry Sawchuk reaches back for the puck, while Toronto's Billy Harris watches and I'm tangled up with Ron Stewart. Sawchuk died in 1970 from injuries incurred following a tussle with Stewart.

that in training camp, because he was a big man, he always did all the skating that the forwards did. He used to take off his goalie pads and beat the majority of the skaters up and down the ice. He was 216-217, so they required him to do the skating.

Terry's weight wasn't a major issue with the team, though. Adams always went out of his way to emphasize that you had to be big and strong enough and if you carried a little extra bit of weight he didn't make a big deal out of it. There were never any directives from Adams to Terry to lose weight.

Terry endured through tremendous pain to play in the NHL. He developed his crouching style in the net due to a broken arm he suffered as a child. It didn't heal properly and left his catching arm shorter than his stick-side arm, so he crouched low in the net to help compensate.

I always got the best of Terry because I kidded him. One of the things I would kid him about was that he was the only guy who combed his hair by moving his head and not his arm. Because of his elbow injury Terry brought his head to the comb. Nobody else ever noticed that, but I used to kid the heck out of him about it. When he got on my case, I'd said, "Okay, Uke," and then I'd mimic him combing his hair.

He's also the only goaltender I ever saw, because of his injury, who would make saves on high shots with his elbow. His arm was all scarred because of that. He was always having issues with that elbow. It really hurt him at times. But he was a kamikaze goaltender. He'd put his head in front of the puck if he had to. He had no fear.

He had bone chips taken out of his elbow in three separate surgeries, and he suffered chest injuries in a 1955 car accident. Over the years, he suffered punctured lungs, a ruptured spleen, a blocked intestine, ruptured disks leading to chronic back pain, a broken instep in his foot, and it was estimated that he took over 600 stitches to his body, the majority in his face. I'll say this—if I had been forced to endure the type of constant physical pain that Terry faced on a daily basis, I'd have thrown the rope over the beam years ago.

His injuries sometimes revolutionized the position. He changed the way the catching glove was made, too. It used to be open in the back until Toronto's Bob Pulford skated across his hand one night and severed his tendons. Toronto trainer Tommy Naylor, who was a good friend of Terry's, made a piece for the glove to cover up that area.

He would play through any injury if he could. During the 1964 playoffs, he checked himself out of hospital, where he'd spent the night in traction after suffering a back injury, and showed up at the rink on game night to shutout the Black Hawks. In Game 7 of that series, Terry was knocked unconscious when he was run over by Chicago forward Reg Fleming. Team physician Dr. Milton Kosey raced to Terry's side and asked him, 'What's two and one?" Terry answered "shoe polish," then passed out again. After trainer Lefty Wilson revived him in the dressing room, Terry told him he knew he was at a hockey game before losing consciousness once more. But by Game 1 of the final series against Toronto, even though he told us he was sore all over, old Ukey was back between the pipes.

In those days, the loss of a goaltender was critical, because you didn't have many. You'd have to pull one up from the system, and sometimes they weren't ready. Still, Terry was always afraid to miss any time in net. He knew that an injury to Lumley had opened the door to his first NHL chance back in 1949-50 and reasoned that if after seeing him in action for just seven games Adams could get rid of Lumley so quickly it could happen to him as well. It did

happen, too. In 1955, Adams shipped Terry to Boston because he had Glenn Hall waiting in the wings. That deal just about broke Terry's heart. He loved Detroit and didn't want to play any place else.

He didn't last two years with the Bruins. He contracted infectious mononucleosis and announced his retirement from the game on January 15, 1957. He said he couldn't sleep or eat and that his nerves were shot, and that he felt like he was letting everyone around him down. Terry started the season at 180 pounds, but by the time he quit, his weight had dropped all the way down to 168 pounds.

That's why I say he had to have been affected long-term by the mono, because he went from 216-217 to 176 pounds and he never gained an ounce after that, regardless of what he ate or drank. He always had a good appetite. I think after the mono, his metabolism changed. He lost all that weight and he never regained it.

The Bruins suspended him, refusing to believe Terry was sick, and this hurt him to the core. The Boston papers called him everything, including a quitter. He talked about suing the papers for libel and I believe deep down the impact of all that negativity really changed his personality for the worse.

135

Toronto's Dick Duff snaps a shot at Terry Sawchuk from close range while I try to get there to help out.

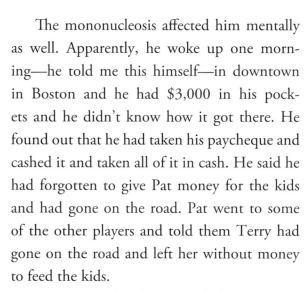

The mononucleosis affected him mentally as well. Apparently, he woke up one morning—he told me this himself—in downtown in Boston and he had $3,000 in his pockets and he didn't know how it got there. He found out that he had taken his paycheque and cashed it and taken all of it in cash. He said he had forgotten to give Pat money for the kids and had gone on the road. Pat went to some of the other players and told them Terry had gone on the road and left her without money to feed the kids.

No matter what the Bruins believed, something was definitely wrong with Terry. When he weighed 176 pounds, he was all bones. He was wide, but he wasn't big, just like a 2 x 10. He looked like a scarecrow. You could see his hip bones sticking out. The man was skinny. His legs had really gotten smaller. If he was in good shape, his legs alone wouldn't let him weigh much less than 200 pounds.

He was also playing poorly, which was unlike Terry. The only time I'd ever seen him struggle during his time in Detroit was during the 1953 Stanley Cup semifinal against Boston. That spring, he gave up soft goals at the wrong time. And once you give up one easy goal, then you get tight on the next one, and then it's an

137

accumulation. And he had never experienced that in his life and at that point in his career he was not ready to cope with it. Terry's big strength was making the big save at the crucial time, and that was missing in that series. If you project forward from that series to the series against Chicago and Montreal in 1967—especially the series against Chicago, when he got hurt—he got beat, but he came back strong. He was able to do that then, because he had gained knowledge from that experience in 1953. He had never learned how to cope with a bad goal or a bad game.

After the series, Terry shouldered the entire blame for the upset loss. That was typical of Sawchuk. He'd take the onus off of other people. "Lay off the hockey club and make me the goat." That was exactly the way Terry was. Terry never blamed anyone for his shortcomings. He never spoke ill of anybody. He never made an enemy.

If Detroit hadn't traded to reacquire his rights from Boston in the summer of 1957, I don't think Terry would have come back to the game. We also would have never grown as friendly as we did, because, the second trip around, after we got Terry back from Boston, that's when we really started to grow close.

I think that we got closer after he was sick. As soon as he came back, that's when we started to room together. There was an affinity between us that just kind of took over. It evolved naturally. We had a lot of fun. We were good companions for one another, because we did not irritate each other. I really understood him.

There is an old fable that when we roomed together on the road, every morning as we'd wake up I'd say good morning to Terry in both French and English. If he answered, we'd talk. If not, there'd be no talking that day. It makes for a great story, but I can tell you it wasn't true. That was all said tongue-in-cheek to demonstrate that he was not always in the best of moods. Why would I say anything to Terry in French? He was grumpy in the morning, but you don't get up and say, "Good morning" to your roommate. You might say, "Do you want to go for breakfast? Well, then get up and get your act together and let's go." I wasn't the most talkative guy in the morning anyway. Terry might not have wanted to say anything, but there were mornings when I didn't want to say anything, either. Besides, I could speak English pretty well. I didn't need to speak French around Terry and I sure didn't tolerate any attitude from him. When he got surly, I told him where he could go. I didn't put up with his crap. I wasn't shy.

To me, there was no change in Terry's personality from when he'd previously been with the Wings, because he was never gruff with me. He was Terry. I took him at face value. I didn't ask what he could do for me, but what I could do to help him?

Terry liked to go out. It was his way of relaxing. One night in Montreal, when Terry was still single, I ran into him and he was with a woman. He introduced me to her and her name was Gerda Munsinger. She wasn't famous then, but years later, she was one of the ones who got caught up in that spy scandal. Two ministers in the cabinet of Conservative Canadian Prime Minister John Diefenbaker admitted to having affairs with Munsinger, who was also accused of being a spy for East Germany, a charge she denied. She was deported in 1961, but a Royal Commission ultimately determined that there had been no breach in security.

Terry was not good with women. And he wasn't good for women. The only relationship that ever lasted for Terry was his relationship with Pat, because she loved him almost blindly. Pat was a pretty straight shooter and a strong

character. I do know that after Terry married Pat, he seemed happier. There was a happy atmosphere. He was eating better, he was keeping better hours. They were soulmates. They loved one another very much, but they fought like cats and dogs. In February of 1958, Pat field for divorce from Terry. He talked to me about it. He felt that it was unjustified and that he could rectify the whole situation, which he did. It was a wake-up call for him.

None of us are perfect and he was far from being perfect, but neither was he the worst person in the world. In his own way, he showed a lot of affection and a lot of love. He'd talk about his kids all of the time. He never said a bad word to me about Pat. It was always his fault. "I screwed up again," he'd say. He was a tremendous teammate and a tremendous competitor and maybe that was his downfall, because he had to have control of his environment and he couldn't quite get it.

As long as I knew Terry—and we played 14 NHL seasons together, a dozen in Detroit and another pair with the Leafs—I didn't realize how much I didn't know about Terry until 1998, when I helped author David Dupuis with his book *Sawchuk: The Troubles and Triumphs of the World's Greatest Goalie.* I'd met

140

David through a mutual friend, NHL scout Paul Henry, and I helped facilitate a meeting between David and the Sawchuk family. Pat and Terry's seven children had never spoken publicly about their life with him before David's book, and the revelations that came out in print were shocking even to someone like me, who'd spent so much time around Terry during his career. I imagine that to finally tell the truth after all those years, it had to be like a cleansing for the family. Whatever the case, I know that their father loved them all in his own way.

It was a story that needed to be told and it needed to be told with both the good and the bad, because I knew healing was necessary. I was gratified to be able to help out in any way I could. It was something that should have been done a lot earlier.

I learned from David's talks with the Sawchuks that Terry was a sometimes-violent alcoholic, a womanizer and definitely not a candidate for father of the year. Pat Sawchuk Milford filed for divorce from Terry three times before finally following through on the fourth petition.

I think Terry's vitriolic relationship with his family was fueled by his personal demons.

He told me that, when he was a kid, his family had problems showing any affection at all. He also saw two of his brothers die before he reached adulthood. This affected him greatly.

But what bothered Terry more than anything else was worry about how he would take care of his family when he was done playing. That played on his mind more and more as he grew closer to the end of his career. He worried about whether he would be able to give them all he could.

Terry was also plagued by a shocking lack of confidence in his own abilities. A lot of people find this hard to believe, but it was true. Even though he won the Vezina Trophy as the NHL's top goalie four times and was a seven-time NHL All-Star choice—three selections to the First Team, four times on the Second Team and he led the NHL in wins five times and in shutouts three times, he was always worried, always looking over his shoulder.

He set NHL records for goaltenders with 103 shutouts, 435 wins and 971 games played, yet feared he wasn't good enough to maintain his position in the NHL. His insecurities tore him apart. The sad thing is that I think Terry would have been so much better had he played today. He would have never had to worry about where the next dollar was going to come from—something we all had to worry about back then, when the money wasn't so good. There would have always been someone ready and willing to give him some kind of work.

Terry loved being a Red Wing. He was familiar with the area, which allowed him to have more of a sense of control. In 1964, when he was taken from Detroit by Toronto in the NHL Intra-League Draft Terry scowled and told me that he wasn't happy, but that he'd report. He always loved playing for the Red Wings and would do anything for the team.

In fact, in 1967, when Roger Crozier, the man who replaced Sawchuk in the Detroit goal in 1964, walked away from the game, insisting

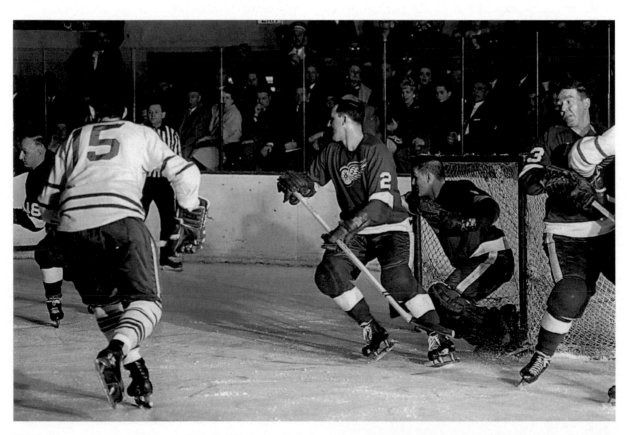

While I keep a Toronto player occupied, Terry Sawchuk, Pete Goegan (2), Gerry Odrowski (18) and Toronto's Billy Harris (15) all follow the path of the puck.

his nerves were shot, Detroit GM Sid Abel approached Terry and asked him if he would speak to Roger. Terry said he would be glad to if Abel thought it would do any good. Like Terry, Roger came back to play hockey again a while later.

Coming back to Detroit, Terry always seemed to find his old form. In his second of three tours with the team he backstopped the Wings to the Stanley Cup final in 1961, 1963 and 1964, though we never could break through and win a Cup any of those years.

142

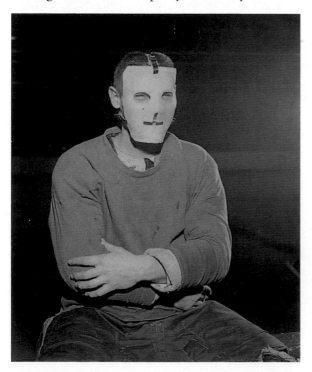

Terry Sawchuk donned a mask in 1961 and felt that it extended his career.

He was really feisty. He was always ready to drop the gloves and go after anybody. He was a real fighter. To him, the puck was never supposed to be in his net, not even when it was crossed the goal line. He always felt he had a chance on a shot. He never felt he was beaten.

He loved to play pinochle and battled constantly to solve the daily *New York Times* crossword puzzle. He was as competitive as they come. I remember a night against the New York Rangers in 1962 when Terry's belligerence led to a real brouhaha and nearly cost me some money. Referee John Ashley assessed Terry a double minor after an altercation around his net with Rangers forward Dave Balon, from which a 15-minute brawl ensued. Val Fonteyne was sent to the box to serve Terry's minors. Making matters worse, the Rangers potted a pair of quick power-play goals. Fonteyne, thinking the two goals had wiped out Sawchuk's two penalties, left the penalty box to head to the Detroit bench, but Ashley ordered him back into the sin bin. I headed straight toward Ashley to argue the point and so did Bill Gadsby. Well, doesn't Ashley assess Bill a game misconduct for bumping into Ashley and me a 10-minute misconduct and $25 fine for arguing the point.

A week later, after an investigation into the incident, NHL president Clarence Campbell ruled that Ashley was wrong and rescinded my fine. Good thing, too. I would have been hitting Terry up for the money, since it was his actions that started the whole thing.

One area where Terry didn't compete was in practice. His main objective during practice was to ensure that the puck never hit him. He'd hug the post on his glove side tightly and wave his stick at the pucks as they went into his net. If someone were foolish enough to get a shot too close to Terry, he'd let him know about it, let me tell you.

He became even less interested in practice as the years passed, especially once we both got to Toronto near the end of his career. Terry reasoned that he only had so many saves left in his battered body, so why waste them in practice? At one end of the ice, we had Johnny Bower, who hated the puck to ever enter his net, practice or no, and down the other end there was Terry, watching them all sail past him. Sometimes, we'd have to stop practice in mid-drill because all the pucks were behind Terry in his net.

He was also a very proud man. During the 1960-61 season, when Abel opted to use Hank Bassen between the pipes more often than Sawchuk, as much as he loved Detroit, Terry asked to be traded. And he posed the question while he was an intermission guest on the broadcast of one of our games. He couldn't stand to be second fiddle.

I remember a night when we were playing in Toronto and that was before they had the high glass. We were killing a penalty and I went to put the puck down the ice and instead, I put it over the glass, hit a kid and smashed his nose. The doctors fixed him up, then we brought him in the dressing room and the first thing that Sawchuk did was walk over to the kid and give him his goalie stick, without the kid even asking. Then he turned to me and said, "If you tell the press about this, I'll kill you. Don't you dare tell a soul about this, you bastard."

Those nice things that he did, he didn't want anyone to talk about, didn't want anybody to say anything at all to anyone. He wanted to help but he didn't want anyone to know. That was Terry. That's the way he was. He liked to present himself as this moody, aloof person, because then people would leave him alone.

As a defenceman, Terry was very easy to play in front of. If you goofed, it was never your fault. Terry would say, "I should have had it." He never blamed anyone else.

He could also make you laugh. He had a great sense of humour, but generally kept that hidden from the public as well. Some nights, Terry used to have to fear his defencemen almost as much as the other team. One night we're leading the Leafs 1-0 going into the third period, and we lose 5-1. I put three in my own net. One went in off my leg, another off my skate, and another off my stick. It was almost comical. Terry was so competitive, I was afraid to go in the dressing room and face him. I really felt badly about it. Well, anyway, I go in, sit down and kind of casual-like say "Geez, Ukey, I put three past you, didn't I?"

144

Terry and I were reunited as teammates with Detroit in 1950-51 when he won the rookie of the year award.

I remember after apologizing to him about the three goals, he just shrugged, looked at me and said: "Yeah, but don't worry, you beat me clean all three times." Believe me, it took a lot to beat Terry Sawchuk, clean or otherwise. He was as competitive a goaltender as ever lived and yet, he never blamed anyone but himself when the puck got past him.

Terry's accomplishments as a goaltender seemed like they would stand forever. His wins total reigned supreme in the NHL for 30 years, and he was the league's shutout king from January 18, 1964 until December 21, 2009. Since then both Patrick Roy and Martin Brodeur have succeeded Terry as the NHL's career wins leaders, while Brodeur has also joined Terry as the only goalie with 100 NHL regular-season shutouts, moving past Terry when he posted his 104th shutout in a 4-0 victory December 21, 2009 over the Pittsburgh Penguins.

I'm not taking anything away from Roy or Brodeur. They are both great goalies. It doesn't bother me that Terry's records have been broken. I just think there are too many teams now and the talent level is too spread out to make a comparison. The shutout record, that's one record I would have never expected anybody to beat. I'm glad it was Marty who did it, though, because as a scout with the New Jersey Devils, I played a role in bringing him to the team, and he's been chiefly responsible for much of the glory we've enjoyed as a franchise over the past two decades. But I still think it's difficult to compare today's goalies to Terry. They've got the big glove now, and all that oversized gear. Terry Sawchuk just had a tiny first basemen's glove, and upper-body padding that was little more than felt.

I remember the night Terry broke the shutout record against the Montreal Canadiens, whom he beat 2-0 at the Forum. Terry had tied the NHL shutout mark earlier that season with a 3-0 win over the Canadiens in Detroit, but it had been overshadowed because that same night Gordie Howe scored his 545th NHL goal to move past another Montreal legend, Maurice (Rocket) Richard, as the league's all-time goal-scoring leader.

Terry made 36 saves that night. He blocked 13 shots in the first period, before Floyd Smith gave the Wings a 1-0 lead. He blocked another 10 pucks during the second period. Then in the third frame, he made 13 more saves, while Eddie Joyal added an insurance goal.

George Hainsworth, winner of the Vezina Trophy the first three seasons it was presented from 1926-27 through 1928-29, had occupied the shutout throne since 1936. Since he'd won all those Vezina Trophies as a member of the Canadiens, naturally, the home team didn't want to see his record fall. Late in the game, though they were down two goals, Canadiens coach Toe Blake still pulled Charlie Hodge, his goalie, and swarmed all over our end. When they pulled Hodge, we thought, "You sons of bitches, you won't give Terry his record, eh? We'll show you." It only made us all madder and we dug down deeper. At the time, it was a record that nobody ever thought would be touched, but Terry did it. We couldn't believe it.

A year after Terry went to Toronto, the Leafs also made a spring move to trade for me. The best thing that ever happened to me was when I got traded to Toronto. Not only did my salary double right away, but I was back playing in front of my friend.

I think it was a good thing for Terry, too. He'd struggled some with the Leafs and didn't seem to be making any friends. His family had stayed behind in Detroit and he was alone in a Toronto apartment. My wife Cindy and I found a home in Mississauga in the west end of Toronto, and we'd often have Terry over for supper. I think it was good for him to have a familiar face around, someone that he could trust.

The early years that we were together in Toronto, I would say that's when Terry was his happiest. In 1965, the first year I was with the Leafs, Pat was down to see him quite often, the family was down to visit quite often. Terry talked about his kids a lot, talked about his family, about Pat coming down, about how she'd cook him a few of his favourite dishes. By the 1960s, I think he'd mellowed a lot.

I'd also help him with his game, too. I'd noticed over the years that whenever Terry's play deteriorated, he'd come up out of his crouch. Once he got back into the habit of playing in his crouch, the old Terry would emerge.

As I have already said, when we won that Cup in Toronto in 67, Terry was his old self, maybe better. Terry was spectacular that spring, sharing the goaltending with Johnny Bower, especially against Chicago, and in his 40-save night in our Cup-deciding 3-1 decision over the Canadiens.

"He came up with the key saves, and gave them the time to get ahead," lamented Canadiens captain Jean Beliveau to the *Canadian Press*. "There were three or four shots in the early part of the game you could usually count on as goals." Added Blake: "The Toronto goaltending (of Sawchuk) in the last two games was exceptional."

Afterward, Terry wasn't exactly celebrating. Asked by *Windsor Star* sports columnist Jack Dulmage what his hockey future held

as the league expanded from six to 12 teams, the goalie who'd just backstopped the Stanley Cup champions doubted there would be much interest in his services. "Aw, who would want me?" he asked.

It turned out the Los Angeles Kings did. They selected him as the first goalie taken in

Terry backstopped the Wings to six Stanley Cup finals and won three of them.

the June 6, 1967 NHL expansion draft. Red Kelly, our teammate in both Detroit and Toronto, was coaching the Kings and was convinced having Terry in net would give them an edge. Terry and I were apart for the last time in our playing days, and his would soon tragically end.

He spent the 1967-68 season in L.A., and then returned for a third stint with Detroit in 1968-69. Acquired by the New York Rangers, Terry's last NHL season was spent as backup to Ed Giacomin with the Rangers in 1969-70.

Shortly after the season ended, there was an incident at the Long Island, N.Y. home shared by Sawchuk and teammate Ron Stewart. While it has never been made clear over the years whether they engaged in fisticuffs, or if it was simply some tomfoolery that got out of hand, Terry fell into a barbecue pit as they scuffled, suffered serious internal injuries and was rushed to hospital. He never recovered and died from a pulmonary embolism at the age of 40 on May 31, 1970, having suffered a bleeding liver and blood clots while hospitalized.

I was at a birthday party for my first wife Cindy that day when news came that Terry had died. Talking to the doctors at Terry's funeral, they said that the mono may have weakened his system and may have caused his liver to enlarge. And his way of living, especially in his last couple of years with the excessive drinking as his marriage to Pat was on its way to ending in divorce, may have made it worse.

I don't remember the last time I talked with Terry, because we never expected something like this to happen, but I do remember the last time I touched him. He was in his coffin and I touched him on one of his big hands.

I served as one of the pallbearers at Terry's funeral when he was buried at Mount Hope Cemetery. I had tears in my eyes. I was shocked. But deep down, I had to admit that Terry's tragic demise wasn't a complete surprise. The way he lived his life, it seemed like he was asking for it.

All these years later, I still think often of my good friend Terry. And when I do, I only ask one question: "Why did he have to go so young?"

Author David Dupuis talks about the role Marcel played in his 1998 book,
Sawchuk: The Troubles and Triumphs of the World's Greatest Goalie.

"Marcel was pivotal, instrumental. Marcel contacted the Sawchuk family for me. A couple of weeks later, the phone rang at work and it was Jerry, Terry's son. He said, 'If Marcel trusts you, then the Sawchuk family trusts you. It's time we did it for closure.' Within two weeks, I was down in Detroit doing interviews. I'm sure none of this ever happens without Marcel's involvement."

BEHIND THE BENCH
MOVING INTO MY SECOND CAREER AS A COACH

MIDWAY THROUGH THE 1968-69 SEASON, Stafford Smythe, club president of the Toronto Maple Leafs, mentioned me in passing. He was primarily being critical of our coach-GM Punch Imlach—Smythe was already greasing the skids to fire Punch at the end of the season—but in the process, he gave an inkling of what my future held.

"A man like Marcel Pronovost should have a player-coaching job in the minors," Smythe said. "He is as knowledgeable a player as you'll find and he should be getting the experience."

As it was, through a combination of injury and Punch wanting to give some of our young kids like Jim Dorey, Pat Quinn, Mike Pelyk and Ricky Ley a good look, I spent a lot of time sitting during the 1968-69 season. I only played in 34 of 76 games.

I could see the writing on the wall in terms of my future with the Leafs, but I felt that I still had some hockey left in me. Other teams agreed. A lot of teams, they were all after me because of my skating ability. The Pittsburgh Penguins were definitely interested in acquiring the services of a veteran defenceman like me and that possibility certainly intrigued me, because of the chance to play alongside my younger brother Jean, who was a right-winger with the team. But the Leafs imposed a $30,000 waiver claim for any seeking to acquire me and no team was willing to pay that kind of stipend for a 39-year-old defenceman who'd endured his share of knee ailments since arriving in Toronto in 1965. I wanted to keep playing. I was resistant to the idea of becoming a minor-league coach, but what choice did I have? My rights belonged to the Maple Leafs.

Leafs general manager Jim Gregory met with my wife Cindy and I to discuss the opportunity. "It's my belief that Pronovost will agree to join Tulsa," Gregory told the Toronto papers on September 11, 1969, the day that the Leafs opened training camp in Peterborough, Ontario. We'd been talking about the job opening through the summer. I was still reluctant about it, though. I wasn't sure I wanted to move my family. In fact, when we went to Gregory's office to finalize the deal and Cindy accompanied me, that was something completely unheard of in those days. She wanted to make sure that we could find a suitable home in Tulsa and the proper schools for our children. It came down to this—if the Tulsa club could convince her that its city could match what we had going for us in Toronto, I figured we could get together on other less important matters such as salary. They convinced her and when all was said and done I signed on the dotted line.

"It's a load off my shoulders," Gregory said. "We had kept the job open for Marcel all

I made my coaching debut with the 1969-70 Tulsa Oilers in the Central League. I'm seated in the front row next to captain Cal Swenson.

summer and would have been in a hole had he turned us down."

Sure, I was originally hesitant about the idea of leaving the NHL. Then when I got involved with the younger kids, I really enjoyed it. It wasn't what I'd originally looked for. I'd hoped instead to get a position as a coach or manager in the NHL because I could see my playing career was coming to an end.

In the minors, I could still take a shift with them, because I was a player-coach, so that helped my own transition into a management role. I played 53 games for Tulsa during the 1969-70 Central Hockey League season.

Working as a player-coach can be a real challenge if you don't have the proper support staff. You had to have cooperation from everybody. Ray Miron, who would later serve in the NHL as GM of the Colorado Rockies and was the guy who hired Don Cherry to coach the Rockies, was GM in Tulsa and helped to run the bench when I took my shifts on the ice. I did it for a couple of years. I coached and I took my turns on defence.

As it turned out, my NHL playing days weren't quite done. When the Leafs arrived in Montreal for a December 10 game against the Canadiens at the Forum, the injury list read

like a who's who of the team's talent. At forward, Dave Keon was out with a thumb injury, Paul Henderson was slowed by a groin ailment, Brit Selby had an eye injury and Ron Ward was sidelined with a knee ailment. It was even worse on the back end, where Ley (knee), Pelyk (collarbone), Quinn (shoulder) and Brian Glennie (knee) were all hurting.

"I'm going to be talking to my minor league coaches, Marcel Pronovost in Tulsa and Alf Pike in Phoenix, to see who is going best before I make mind on who to call up," Leafs coach John McLellan told the Toronto media.

The Leafs recalled two of my defencemen, Gord Nelson and Chris Evans, for back to-back 6-3 losses at Montreal and Philadelphia. Then they opted to add some veteran support. I got the call for a December 13 game against the Detroit Red Wings. When we won 3-1 the next night at Madison Square Garden over the New York Rangers, I'd played three games in three nights and covered over 2,000 miles of travel in that span. Not bad for a 39-year-old defenceman.

Nelson spoke highly of my work as a mentor to the Toronto media during his three-game stint with the Leafs. "I'm in a pretty good spot in Tulsa with Marcel Pronovost

153

coaching," Nelson explained. "He's teaching me a lot. Marcel always played a thinking game in the National Hockey League and I think he's teaching me to play the same kind of game."

A lot of the guys I groomed in Tulsa ended up playing for the Leafs as regulars, players like forwards Billy MacMillan, Denis Dupere, Brian Spencer, Errol Thompson and Rick Kehoe, defencemen Quinn, John Grisdale, Joe Lundrigan and Brad Selwood, and goalies Ron Low and Gord McRae. We also had Rene Robert, whom I later coached in Buffalo and who was part of the Sabres' famous French Connection line with Gilbert Perreault and Richard Martin. That period of time, it was a real transition phase for the Leafs. They were restocking to replace all of us veterans who'd won the Cup in 1967. There was opportunity for young talent and the players that you had, if they did what they were supposed to do, they got promoted.

While I was up with the Leafs for that seven-game farewell tour, the Soviet Union's national team was in Toronto and two of the players, Anatoli Firsov and Igor Romishevsky, watched what turned out to be my final NHL game against St. Louis from a perch in the director's box at Maple Leaf Gardens. As we beat the Blues 4-1, they had many questions for two of our injured players, Quinn and Glennie, who were also seated in the director's box.

Quinn told me later that they'd asked about me. They wanted to know about me. They recognized me as a very good NHL player. Quinn said it took him an hour through an interpreter to explain that I was only up with the team as an emergency replacement due to injuries and was actually coaching Toronto's farm team in Tulsa. Quinn said that they also asked him when NHL teams would play against the Russians.

Nobody could speak Russian, so we didn't really get to talk the game with them, but I was anxious to play against them, and I'm disappointed that I never got the chance. I would have liked to crush a few of them with some of my hits. That eight-game 1972 Summit Series when the NHL players rallied from a 1-3-1 deficit to beat the Russians 4-3-1, really changed the approach to the game in terms of things such as off-ice conditioning. Some players took advantage of it, and the guys that didn't want to got left behind.

In terms of the style of hockey played on the ice, I was more inclined to play the old game. Dump it in, chase it. It was more suited

154

to my style, because it tended to lead to a more physical game. There wasn't a lot of hitting in the European game in those days.

I didn't get to play against the Russians, but I did get a little taste of European hockey prior to the start of the 1969-70 season. A group from the Maple Leafs—captain George Armstrong, goalie Johnny Bower, chief scout Bob Davidson, a Leafs captain in the 1940s, and I all travelled to Germany to conduct a hockey school for 400 Canadian boys, children of Canadian soldiers stationed in military bases there. NHL officials Matt Pavelich and Dutch van Deelan also participated in the camp.

The 1971-72 season I stepped away from the ice into a full-time coaching position, and there was plenty of talk while I was coaching the Oilers that NHL teams were interested in my services. When the Montreal Canadiens won the Stanley Cup in 1970-71, they'd replaced head coach Claude Ruel with Al MacNeil, and even though they won, the Canadiens experienced some of the same problems that the franchise endured during the 2011-12 season after they'd fired Jacques Martin and hired Randy Cunneyworth.

The fans, the French-language media and even some of the players—most notably Henri Richard—spoke out against MacNeil, demanding that a French-speaking man be installed behind the bench. And one of the guys being suggested for the job was me.

Montreal, they contacted me, but it had to be done away from the rink, because I was still working for the Leafs. But in the end it just ended up being a rumour. It never went that far and they ended up hiring Scotty Bowman, which worked out well for the franchise. They won five Stanley Cups between 1972-79 with Scotty as coach of the Canadiens.

I wouldn't have wanted to play for Scotty. He's too much his own boss. Imlach, I could handle, because of my experience. And yet I probably would have been the type of player that would have appealed to Scotty. He liked veteran players. His early expansion teams in St. Louis utilized veterans like Glenn Hall and Jacques Plante in goal, Al Arbour and Doug Harvey on defence and Dickie Moore up front. The Blues kind of followed Toronto's blueprint, and it seemed to work for them. They played in three straight Stanley Cup Finals from 1968-70.

There was some speculation the following season in Toronto that I was going to be the next coach of the Leafs, but that was all rumour

as well. That talk all started when McLellan was ill during the 1971-72 season and it was uncertain whether he'd be back behind the bench. But McLellan regained his health and returned to the job.

I landed my first big-league head coaching job in 1972 and it came in an entirely new league. The World Hockey Association was born as a rival to the NHL and for the first time in decades, players had choices when it came time to decide where they were going to play. On July 6, 1972, I was announced as head coach of the fledgling Chicago Cougars by Ed Short, the club's GM. It was a pretty hard choice to break 22 years of ties with the NHL, but it was the right choice for me at the time.

I think I could have played in that league. I thought about playing in the WHA. It was difficult decision to leave the NHL after all those years, but they paid you good money to jump to the WHA. A lot of guys looked at it as their chance to show they could play in the big leagues and some of the older players saw it as an opportunity to play a few more years and make top money. It was also really the first chance where players had some control over their future and had options as far as where they could ply their trade as hockey players.

I made my major-league coaching debut with the Chicago Cougars during the inaugural season of the WHA in 1972-73. Left-winger Jim Benzelock (22) waits for his next turn on the ice.

Like most of those original WHA teams, our roster was littered with interesting characters. Former Chicago Black Hawks tough guy Reggie Fleming was probably our most well-known player. We had journeymen defencemen such as Larry Cahan and Larry Mavety. Rosaire Paiement was another well-respected scrapper and former Detroit Red Wing. Ed Hatoum's claim to fame was that he was the first NHL player born in Lebanon. I even brought along two of my Tulsa players to Chicago—forwards Jan Popiel and Bob Liddington.

We also had a couple of European players in camp that fall, Swedish forwards Benny Andersson and Ulf Sterner. Sterner was the more well-known of the two, a star in Sweden who'd won a world title with the Swedes in 1962 and an Olympic silver medal in 1964. He'd even become the first European-trained player to skate in the NHL when he suited up for four games with the New York Rangers during the 1964-65 season. I had actually played a game against him on January 31, 1965. We went into Madison Square Garden and gave Sterner and the Rangers a real pounding by a 4-1 count. We hit Sterner every chance we got. The next season, he opted to return to play in Sweden.

It didn't work out this time, either. We released both of the Swedish players during our training camp in Hibbing, Minnesota for disciplinary reasons. Both had broken training rules several times and as far as I was concerned, if a man can't take care of himself, then I'm not going to babysit him.

Another fellow who got his start with the Cougars and came to make quite a name for himself was the fellow I hired as my assistant coach, Jacques Demers. I was friends with Jacques Beauchamp, a sportswriter in Montreal who was a big fan of Jacques and he had mentioned Demers' name to me as a possible coaching candidate. I kind of had Jacques in my thoughts, but I also had Larry Cahan in mind before that. In the end, I made up my mind to go with Demers. Jacques was 27 at the time and had coached a number of hockey teams, including a junior club in Chateauguay.

I called Jacques and asked him if he was interested in a job as my assistant coach. He accepted, and it was certainly a starting point for him. Jacques later became a head coach with the WHA's Indianapolis Racers and after the NHL and WHA merged in 1979; he coached the Quebec Nordiques, the St. Louis Blues, the Detroit Red Wings, the Tampa Bay

Lightning and led the Canadiens to their most recent Stanley Cup triumph in the spring of 1993.

The key to success for any hockey team is having the right rapport between the coach and his players. Jacques could certainly create his end of it. He believes in people. This is how he can get the best out of them. But the one thing he needed was the right people in the dressing room to help him.

His personality had a lot to do with it. A coach's personality will eventually show through in his hockey club. Jacques Demers is a guy who believes in himself. He's a blue-collar type of guy, a guy who is always looking for ways to improve himself as a person and in his profession, a guy who believes in honesty.

Today, Jacques serves as a member of the Canadian Senate, as does Frank Mahovlich. So a couple of my old hockey buddies are now Senators—the kind who work for the government in Ottawa and not those playing hockey in the same city in the NHL.

Perhaps the most curious thing in Chicago was our home, the 9,000-seat International Ampitheatre. Located on the south side of Chicago immediately next to the Union Stock Yards, you can imagine what the neighborhood

smelled like. Opened in 1934, Elvis Presley and the Beatles both played there, former world heavyweight champion Joe Frazier's last bout was fought there, and five US Presidential conventions were held there, including the infamous 1968 Democratic nomination of Hubert Humphrey, where rioting during protests against the Vietnam War led to the arrest and trial of the legendary Chicago Seven, including Abbie Hoffman, Jerry Rubin and Tom Hayden, who was once married to Jane Fonda.

The rink had a portable ice surface, so you could actually hear the ice crack under your skates when you moved around. Our largest crowd of the season was 9,197, which was nearly 200 above seating capacity at the old rink, when the Winnipeg Jets and long-time Chicago Black Hawks star Bobby Hull came to town for the first time. Hull didn't disappoint the crowd, blasting home four goals as the Jets beat us 7-2. Bobby was familiar with the area. A cattle rancher in the off season, when he was with the Black Hawks, Bobby displayed his award-winning cattle stock next door to the rink in the stockyards.

The game succinctly summed up our season. We couldn't score at all, finishing last in the league with 245 goals, and missed the playoffs with a 26-50-2 record. I only lasted one year in Chicago, which was probably a good thing. Pat Stapleton, another former Black Hawks player, took over from me and eventually put together a group of players to purchase the franchise. But in the spring of 1975 the franchise folded.

While one team I was associated with was vanishing, another one was being reborn. I was invited to Windsor Arena the night of September 24, 1975 to attend the inaugural game of the Windsor Spitfires' return to The Ontario Hockey Association's Major Junior A Series, the same league in which I'd played for the Spitfires during the late 1940s. That Windsor team had come to the city from Galt in the fall of 1947, my first season with the club, and had relocated to Hamilton following the 1952-53 season.

Others who were there that night from the old guard were Lloyd Pollock, the team's GM,

Tulsa forwards Doug Acomb (21) and Rene Robert (17) listen to my instructions. Robert would later play for me in Buffalo on the French Connection line with Gilbert Perreault and Richard Martin.

and former teammates Doug McKay, Gord Haidy, Ivan Walmsley and Bruce Giesebrecht. It was nice to visit my old stomping ground at Windsor Arena. Soon, I'd be back in junior hockey on a regular basis. Later that year, the Hull Festivals of the Quebec Major Junior Hockey League hired me as head coach.

I liked coaching the junior ranks. You had better control over your guys, because they respected you more. Coaching in the minor pros was tough. You'd get on a roll and someone would get called up, someone else would get sent down and you'd have to juggle your lineup. In junior, you had control over who was in your lineup. But you have to accept that as your role as a minor-pro coach. You are there to develop players for the NHL. If they go up to the big leagues and succeed that means you've done your job. You are as much a teacher as a coach in the minors, and even more so in the junior ranks.

In my first game as coach in Hull, we fell behind 5-1 against Sherbrooke, then staged an amazing rally for a 9-7 win. We didn't have a lot of pro-calibre talent in Hull. Glen Sharpley was our only player who went on to have any sort of success in the NHL. He was a first-round pick of the Minnesota North Stars, and

his career was ended prematurely by an eye injury.

It was a tough go in Quebec at that time. You had all the better juniors in the OHA. For a long time, the Montreal Junior Canadiens were in the OHA, so many of the best French-Canadian players would be playing in Ontario. Even my brother Jean, he played in Ontario and won the Memorial Cup with the Niagara Falls Flyers in 1964-65. That's his claim to fame. I got the Stanley Cups, he got the Memorial Cup. It's not hard to understand why there was such a long drought between Memorial Cup wins for teams from Quebec. The Quebec Remparts, led by Guy Lafleur, won it in1970-71 and no Quebec-based team won it again until the Granby Predateurs in 1995-96.

I'd completed my third season in Hull and was getting ready for training camp in early August of 1977 when I got a call from an old boss. Imlach, my coach when we won the Stanley Cup a decade earlier in Toronto, was now GM of the Buffalo Sabres and he wanted me as his new coach.

To tell the truth, I wasn't certain as to whether I wanted the job. It was Hull GM Norm Baril who pushed me into shuffling off to Buffalo. I liked Hull. I was well treated and

I didn't envision moving on to the NHL. I doubt very much if I would have accepted the job if Norm hadn't encouraged me to go. And I don't think I would have considered going anywhere but Buffalo, because Punch and I had always respected each other and got along well.

I was aware that Punch had been scouting my work for some time. He'd sent John Anderson, his right-hand man, to Hull to watch several of our games during the 1976-77 season. I knew Anderson wasn't there to scout our players, because as I said before, we weren't exactly loaded with NHL prospects.

"The main ingredient I was looking for was a man strong enough to make the players play as a team and not how they wanted to play," Imlach told the media after hiring me. "Pronovost is a winner and that's very important. He's a teaching coach. He coached juniors and developed players for a number of years. He has lots of experience, knows the game and is bilingual. Our French players won't be able to put anything over on him."

I made my NHL debut as a head coach with the Buffalo Sabres in 1977-78. We won 44 games and finished second in the Adams Division.

I had some familiarity with the Buffalo roster. Forwards Brian Spencer, Don Luce and Rene Robert had all played for me when I was coaching Tulsa in the Central League. We enjoyed a solid 1977-78 season, my first as an NHL coach, losing just twice in our first 11 games. Among the highlights of those first games was a 3-2 win over the Flyers at the Spectrum. The Sabres had gone 0-15-2 in Philly prior to that, but to me, it wasn't a big deal. I didn't even bring the subject up. You can't go yelling and screaming about a streak in a building. All that does is put it in their minds more. To me, the interesting thing about the game was that I was facing an old rival behind the Flyers' bench. When I first got into coaching with Tulsa in 1969, Philadelphia coach Fred Shero, the mastermind behind Philadelphia's Broad Street Bullies teams that won back-to-back Stanley Cups in 1973-74 and 1974-75, was coaching in Omaha.

Of our 19 ties, six were against the Pittsburgh Penguins, who were coached by Johnny Wilson, my old friend and teammate in Shawinigan, Windsor and Detroit. "There's only one way to explain it," Johnny suggested to reporters. "Marcel and I have too much respect and admiration for one another, we can't stand it if one or the other of us win, so

163

My old Toronto bench boss Punch Imlach was GM in Buffalo in 1977 when he hired me for my first NHL coaching job as the man in charge of the Sabres.

we have to settle for a tie each time." I guess you could say that the Wilsons and I had deep-rooted ties.

We ended the regular season going 44-17-19 and finished second to Boston in the Adams Division. After taking care of the New York Rangers in the opening round of the playoffs, we drew the Flyers in the quarter-finals. This time, there was no win in Philly for us in the cards. We lost all three games of the series that were played there and ended up losing the best-of-seven set in five games.

I'd always gotten along well with Punch when he coached me with the Leafs and there was a similar respect when I coached for him. He never told me who not to play. He never gave me any orders.

Things didn't go nearly as well the following season. We opened by winning just twice in the first 10 games and never could seem to put a run together. After back-to-back losses to Montreal during the first weekend in December, Sabres president Seymour Knox announced that both Punch and I were fired. Punch had run the team since the franchise first joined the NHL in 1970.

I wasn't happy about losing my job, but I understood the way the game worked. You can't fire all the players. It's easier to fire the coach and the GM. That's life. You're hired to be fired. But in actuality, I was hoping that they would have given me a bit more of an opportunity. I felt like the team was showing signs of coming out of its slump and I wish that I'd had a little more time to work with them and try to get it turned around. I'm not bitter, though. I went to the school of hard knocks.

I wasn't out of work for long. Hull was once again in the market for a coach and they hired me for a second tour behind their bench

on December 18, 1978. The team had a new nickname now, the Olympiques. I was happy to be back. My first love had always been junior hockey. It's quite a challenge coaching the kids. As you see the youngsters progressing and think of a couple of them making it to the NHL you get a real feeling of satisfaction. I played the game long enough so that I felt I could teach someone else.

We had some players in Hull this time around who'd go on to do well as NHLers. One was John Chabot, a play-making centre who went on to enjoy a solid NHL career,

I had two stints as coach of Hull in the QMJHL sandwiched around my time in Buffalo.

including stints with Pittsburgh and the Red Wings. On defence, we had Alain Vigneault, who was team captain. His playing career in the NHL wasn't sensational, but he's certainly done well since moving into the coaching ranks. Vigneault led the Vancouver Canucks to consecutive President's Trophy wins in 2010-11 and 2011-12 and guided the Canucks to Game 7 of the 2011 Stanley Cup final before they fell to Boston.

He was a clever kid and a quick study. Alain liked the odd beer and he's a good-looking kid. Girls were always around him, but he wasn't a discipline problem and he never lied. He was an easy kid to coach.

There was speculation during the summer of 1979 that I would be named the next coach of the Maple Leafs. Punch had returned as GM in Toronto and everyone assumed he'd bring his old friend Marcel along with him as coach. But once again, all the talk was nothing more than rumours.

Just like with my previous turn in Hull, I would leave when the NHL came calling again. And once again, my trip back to the big leagues would be thanks to another long-time acquaintance from my hockey days. Ted Lindsay had been named GM of the Red Wings in 1977

and in his first season led them to their first playoff berth since 1970 and their first playoff series win since 1966. But just like in Buffalo, things went sour in 1978-79. The following season Lindsay brought me in as an assistant coach to Kromm. When things didn't turn around he dismissed Kromm and took over as coach himself. But even though Ted was listed as coach, I handled the bench during games and ran the practices.

The players came around and gave me their support. All I told them was that I hadn't scored any goals from behind the bench and I hadn't prevented any. If we were going to get things going, it was up to them. They had to believe in themselves. I've always been of the opinion that an athlete's biggest enemy is insecurity and apprehension. You need to feel secure before things will get better.

I felt that there was a good nucleus of players in Detroit, guys like forwards Dale McCourt and Mike Foligno and defence-man Reed Larson. And it sure started off on the right foot. We went into Vancouver and whipped the Canucks 5-2 in our first game in charge. Vaclav Nedomansky scored twice and the win moved us to 15th overall and back into a playoff position. But then we skidded, losing

165

Ted Lindsay brought me back to Detroit in 1980 to work as his assistant coach with the Red Wings.

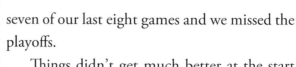

seven of our last eight games and we missed the playoffs.

Things didn't get much better at the start of the 1980-81 campaign. Ted had moved in behind the bench to join me, but we were stumbling along at 3-14-13, including an 0-12-1 road record, when both Lindsay and I were let go.

Even though things didn't work out in Detroit, returning to town, that was fun. It had been quite a few years in between the time that my playing days as a Red Wing came to an end in 1965, but the game was the same. It was nice to come back to an area that I knew and that I considered my second home. I understood the pressure that had been placed on Ted's shoulders. It's hard to work the two jobs. He needed some help. He had everything on his plate. Sure, the outcome wasn't what we wanted, but you take it in stride. At the time, the situation warranted it. I'm still a diehard Red Wing. I spent 18 years in the organization and you can't forget that. Besides, being bitter is a waste of time.

The homecoming continued that spring, when I was offered the opportunity to take charge of another of my old clubs. The Spitfires were looking for a new coach, and on May 27,

167

1980-81 was my second season as assistant coach of the Red Wings.

1981, they hired me to take over the reins. The Windsor job was a case of perfect timing. I was in the area and the job became available. As I've said before, I loved coaching juniors, working with 16-18-year-old players. The big thing with these young people is to keep it simple and evolve from a simple positional system. To me, the biggest reward as a coach is seeing a smile on a player's face when something you taught him works. I was 17 when I first came to Windsor and I lived here when I played for the Wings, so I guess I was coming home in a way. I've certainly always viewed Windsor as my adopted home.

"He's a total professional in every way, and there's no question about his hockey knowledge," Spitfires owner Fred Sorrell told *The Windsor Star*. "He's been a winner and he can bring nothing but experience and know-how to our organization. Marcel discussed discipline and teaching in a way that impressed me. We seem to be on the same wavelength."

As a coach, I liked to tailor my style to the players I had. If I had a choice, though, I'd want forecheckers and skaters blended with aggressiveness. If you haven't got the puck, there's one sure way of getting it back—hit someone.

With Windsor, just like Detroit, I was coming back to another team that I'd played

for. That's why I came back, but they paid for it. The first season in Windsor, we endured a 20-game losing streak. We still got into the playoffs, but were swept aside quickly by the Kitchener Rangers. We did have some solid players, future NHLers such as forwards Paul MacDermid, Claude Loiselle and Paul Lawless and defenceman Craig Muni.

The next season, disaster struck. If it wasn't for bad news, there wouldn't have been any news to report about our start to the 1981-82 Ontario Hockey League season. The Spitfires lost our first nine games and after a 6-5 overtime loss in Sudbury to the Wolves, I was assessed a gross misconduct, accused of making verbal overtures toward referee Bob Morley and kicking the door to the officials' dressing room. I was suspended indefinitely by OHL commissioner Dave Branch.

After my hearing, I was handed a 10-game suspension. The team continued to struggle in my absence and when the Spitfires dropped to 2-13 halfway through my suspension, I was fired as coach. I still feel that Branch overreacted to the situation in terms of the length of the suspension, but I left with no shame. I did everything according to my conscience. I met with the players one last time and told not to

I'd come full circle in the junior ranks when I was hired to coach the Windsor Spitfires in 1981-82.

be angry or hurt, but to just dig down deep and continue to do their jobs.

It looked like that might be it for my coaching career. I held no bitterness, though. There's always a difference of opinion when you're a coach. There were a couple of places where I felt that I didn't get a decent break, but things are better left unsaid. When you start throwing mud in the air, a little bit of it will fall on you, too. It's better to let sleeping dogs lie.

I worked during 1983-84 season as an assistant coach to Chris Coury with the Detroit Little Caesars midgets and that summer got a call out of the blue from the Belle River Canadiens of the Great Lakes Junior C Hockey League. A town east of Windsor, there was a long-standing hockey tradition, but success had eluded the team, which had never won a championship. They named me coach of the team.

People questioned whether Belle River was a stopgap destination for me, but that wasn't the case at all. I treated it as I had any of my jobs, a challenge to do the very best I could.

That was one of the most fun years I ever had in the game of hockey. The guys responded so well. I'd say, "You do this," or "You do that," and they would do it. That was the most

focused group of young men I've ever worked with. All I had to do was give them a little advice and open the gate.

Being so young, they didn't remember me as a player, but I skated with them, so they knew I had some skill. I don't know if all of them knew of my significance as an NHL player, but Tie Domi certainly did.

Domi hailed from Belle River and tried out for the team on a lark as a 14-year-old. He'd only been playing hockey for four years at the time. He was a diamond in the rough, but boy was he tough. He turned 15 during the season, but all the 20-year-olds in the league were scared of him. He'd fight anybody. He played a lot on that team and he earned every minute. He was like quite a few guys on that team who came up through the local minor hockey ranks.

Domi had that aggressive streak in him and he wanted to learn and was willing to do whatever it took to get better. I recommended Domi to Peterborough Petes coach Dick Todd, who took him in the OHL draft. At the time, I would have never thought that Tie would go on to accomplish all he did as an NHL player, playing more than 1,000 games in the league, the majority of them with one of my old teams, the Maple Leafs. But he used the tools that he had to great success. He took advantage of his toughness to make a home for himself in the lineup and I give him credit for it. He made the most of the abilities he had.

Whatever you might have thought about Domi as a player, he belonged in the NHL. He earned it. He got there because he was willing to play tough. He understood the tools he had in his belt and he used those tools to make it. That was his way, and as long as that style is an accepted part of hockey, all power to the kid. Filling the role of tough guy, it's more than just having the guts to fight. You need to be a solid person inside. It's an extremely difficult role to fill because of the pressure. Away from the ice, Tie is no barbarian. His hobbies include chess and croquet. He's like a teddy bear. Gentle as a lamb, and he had the support of a strong family.

As a coach, it gives you a great deal of self-satisfaction, because you're the one who planted the seed that eventually grew into that player. You wait until he shows the signs that he wants it. That was it with Domi. He was willing to do whatever it took to get there.

That Belle River squad really captured the spirit of hockey fans in the community. We won the league title for the very first time in club history and moved on to play Midland for the Ontario Hockey Association Junior C title. I couldn't go anywhere in the streets without people stopping me and asking about the team and how things were going.

We beat Midland 4-1 in a best-of-seven series, taking the title game by a 4-2 verdict in their rink. As the celebration continued, I went and took a seat by myself on the bus. I didn't want it to be about me. This win was for the kids. They deserved the attention. They worked hard, did what was asked of them and were rewarded.

It was kind of funny when you think about it. I thought about all those years that my father Leo had devoted to supporting the Montreal Canadiens before I made the NHL and now here I was, leading Canadiens of a different sort to a championship. It was my first title win since I captured the Stanley Cup with the Leafs in 1967.

I believed that I still had a contribution to make at the higher levels of the game. I had studied the game at all levels. I thought I could be of help to an NHL team, maybe not as a head coach, but in an assistant's role, or perhaps in the areas of personnel or scouting.

The game was about to agree with me.

172

Tie Domi talks about playing for Marcel Pronovost:

"I tried out for the Belle River Canadiens just shy of my 15th birthday. I never expected to make it and I still recall when Marcel told me I'd earned a spot. He said: 'This is why you made it,' and tapped his chest over his heart. I never forgot that. Just getting the chance to meet a Hall of Famer like Marcel was a thrill in itself, but to be able to learn the game from him was unbelievable. That season, everybody contributed. Different people stepped up at different times to score the big goal, to make the key play. Belle River is where it all started for me. It will always be the place where I'm from. It will always be the town I call home."

My three Stanley Cup rings that I earned as a scout with the New Jersey Devils.

A DEVIL OF A TIME
BIRD-DOGGING THE FUTURE OF THE GAME
LEADS TO MORE STANLEY CUP GLORY

IN AUGUST OF 1985, after much soul-searching, I accepted a position as the coach of the newly formed Windsor Bulldogs Junior B hockey club. It was a difficult choice, because I'd enjoyed my time with the Belle River Canadiens the previous season. The people in Belle River had been so wonderful that I had intended to give them another year.

Two things ultimately made my mind up for me. One was when the Bulldogs affiliated with the Windsor Compuware Spitfires of the Ontario Hockey League, and the other was the chance to work with Bulldogs general manager Skeets Harrison. I always liked Skeets. I enjoy a good hockey man and I think he was a very good hockey man. Lots of times, I kidded him that we'd make a good team. That's what swung me over.

I'd interviewed that summer with a couple of teams about coaching positions, the Sudbury Wolves of the OHL and the Toledo Goaldiggers of the International Hockey League, but neither opportunity came to pass. Though I didn't know it at the time I was soon to get a call from an old employer that would dramatically change the direction of my hockey career.

Not long after I'd accepted the position with the Bulldogs, Jim Gregory, who was the GM in Toronto when I got my first coaching job in Tulsa, called me and asked if I'd be interested in a job with the NHL's Central Scouting Bureau. Ron Harris, an old teammate of mine with the Detroit Red Wings, he'd left the bureau to accept an assistant coaching position with the Quebec Nordiques, so there was an opening. Even though I'd taken the Bulldogs job, I did have an out in my contract if a pro job came up and this position, it was a job in the NHL, so I didn't think I could turn it down.

Working with Central Scouting is somewhat different than other scouting. When you're working for a specific team, you're scouting for players that can make your team better, help you win games. With Central Scouting at the time, there were 12 of us scouting and you're working for all the teams, assessing the available talent that is eligible for that year's NHL entry draft, so you're trying to give them a handle on who are the best players out there in each draft year.

Scouting certainly was nothing new to me. When I coached in Tulsa, I had to go out on the road after the season was over and scout for more players. When I coached in junior, every day off you got, you had to go out and see what talent there was. There are similarities between coaching and scouting. Each is about finding the talent. On the one side, as a scout, you're looking for talent. On the other side, as a coach, you're looking to exploit that talent. Of all the jobs I've performed in hockey, the easiest was as a player. When that is your job, there's only one person you have to worry about.

I liked scouting right away. I had gotten tired of coaching for a number of reasons, the first of which was the daily stress of the job. With scouting, you weren't under the day-to-day pressure to win and you met a lot of nice people while on the road. I would run across a lot of hockey people I'd gotten to know over the years. They all loved to talk hockey and the

conversations were invigorating. It didn't matter if you were reminiscing about the old days, or getting into deep discussion about the inside aspects of the game today. Either way, it was a pleasurable experience.

I can tell you that scouting was a lot different in those days. There was no Internet, no computer work and certainly not the video analysis like there is today. Today, nobody gets missed. Nobody falls through the cracks. We do a lot of video work and our network of scouts covers the entire hockey world. It's a year-round job now with all of the summer tournaments.

One thing hasn't changed, though, and that's the travel involved with the work. In a typical week, I might start out at home in Windsor, but my work could take me right across Canada and the United States. I scouted all three major junior leagues—the OHL, Western and Quebec Major Junior Hockey Leagues—the Tier II leagues and the US college and high school games. Sometimes, you could go two weeks with a game every night.

Here's what a typical slate might be like: a Wednesday game in Guelph, Thursday in Windsor, then Friday in Kitchener. Saturday, perhaps an NCAA game in Bowling Green,

Ohio, Sunday in London, then Monday back to Windsor. Tuesday, I'd pack my bags and head to the airport to check out the goings-on in the Western part of Canada. I'd be in Calgary, then Medicine Hat, then on to Winnipeg for a few Tier II games, then down to Duluth, Minnesota for more NCAA games, and then back through Regina, Saskatoon and on to Victoria and Seattle, Washington to get looks at more WHL players. After that, I'd come back to Windsor, do a few games in Ontario, then I was back on the highway to check out Quebec. You needed a reliable car and strong resolve. Sure, it may seem like a heavy schedule to many people, but after all those years in hockey, it is very hard to quit the game and get out. The game gets in your blood and the love affair never dies.

One thing I like to do for fun is I look back to 1946 and try to picture who the guys were that would have been drafted first overall if they had a draft back in those days. I kind of go through every season and look at who might have been the top picks in those seasons if the draft had existed then. In fact, the draft wasn't introduced by the NHL until 1963 and really didn't become a significant part of team-building until after the 1967 expansion of the league from six to 12 teams.

But think about it. Try to put yourself in the shoes of a hockey scout. In 1946, the top available players were Gordie Howe, Bill Gadsby, Fern Flaman, Howie Meeker, Gus Mortson and Cal Gardner. In my first season, besides me, you could choose from among the Wilson brothers, Red Kelly, Bill Barilko and Don Raleigh. Or how about 1957? Who would you take with the first draft pick—Bobby Hull,

Posing with Jimmy Peters and Bill Quackenbush at a Red Wings alumni game.

Frank Mahovlich or Stan Mikita? It makes for interesting debates.

In the summer of 1990, after working with Central Scouting for five years, I accepted a scouting position with the New Jersey Devils. It was one of the best decisions of my hockey career. The best years, really, have been since I've joined the Devils. Working with Devils GM Lou Lamoriello, it's so enjoyable. He's such a competent man and he's very loyal to his employees. We have a good group, but it's a team effort, from scouting director and executive vice-president of hockey operations David Conte on down.

We've won three Stanley Cups since I joined New Jersey's staff—in 1995, 2000 and 2003—and the work of the scouting staff is evident on the roster of each of those Cup-winning teams. Our 1995 team included New Jersey draftees such as defenceman Scott Niedermayer and Bruce Driver and forwards John MacLean, Bill Guerin, Sergei Brylin and Brian Rolston. In 2000, our homegrown talent included Niedermayer, defencemen Colin White and Brad Bombardir and forwards Brylin, Jay Pandolfo, Steve Brule, Krzysztof Oliwa, Patrik Elias, John Madden and Scott Gomez. Elias, Madden, Gomez, Brylin, Pandolfo and White were still key players in our 2003 win and the

newcomers included forward Brian Gionta and defenceman Brian Rafalski. Michael Rupp, who scored our Cup-winning goal in 2003, was a guy I'd seen playing for the Spitfires that we drafted 76th overall in 2000.

In 2012, even though we lost the final to the Los Angeles Kings, several of our key players were again products of our system, such as forwards Elias, Sykora, Zach Parise, Travis Zajac, David Clarkson and Adam Henrique and defenceman Andy Greene. Henrique, I saw him right in my own backyard as he won two

Adam Henrique, here celebrating his overtime winning goal in the 2009 Memorial Cup semifinals, was a key player in the New Jersey Devils' 2012 Stanley Cup run.

180

Posing with the Stanley Cup and my good friend, former NHL defenceman and longtime Northeastern coach Fernie Flaman. I won my first Stanley Cup with Detroit in 1950 and Fernie won it the next season with Toronto.

Memorial Cups with the Windsor Spitfires. One thing that I liked about him right away was that he's not afraid to play defence. He doesn't care who gets the points. He knows he'll get his share. The thing that has always impressed me the most is his willingness to share. He never takes the credit for himself.

Of course, there's one key element in all of those teams that I've yet to mention, the man who has been the foundation of the New Jersey franchise for the past two decades, our 1990 first-round pick, goalie Martin Brodeur. He's been the key to our success story and I'm proud to say I was sold on him from the beginning. I lobbied hard for us to take him with our first pick of that draft year. We were actually able to trade down on draft day that year, exchanging picks with Calgary. The Flames used the No. 11

pick, which had been ours, to take a goalie as well, Trevor Kidd. Nine picks later, we selected Brodeur. I don't need to tell you which goalie made a larger impact as an NHLer.

During the 2012 playoffs, when New Jersey eliminated Philadelphia, one scout remarked that the difference between the two teams was the Devils had suited up the same goalie for 20 years, while the Flyers spent those 20 years searching for a goalie.

The first time I saw Martin play was in Montreal when he was in the QMJHL with the St. Hyacinthe Laser. They weren't a great team—they barely made the playoffs that season, but he played sensationally that night. He was so poised, even at a young age. His numbers and successful career remind me of Terry Sawchuk, but his composure and his mannerisms and easy-going, positive personality are more like Johnny Bower. Marty is unique in the way he plays the game, too. He never went for the butterfly style of goaltending so popular in Quebec. His style is more open to evolution and innovation and I think that's why he's been both so successful and as enduring as an elite netminder. He's an old-school-style goalie in that he's played at least 70 games in a dozen of his NHL seasons and has started 194

consecutive playoff games in New Jersey's net. Brodeur has been to the Devils what Gordie Howe was to the Red Wings, absolutely the most important piece of the puzzle.

During my playing days, I won four Stanley Cups thanks to the goaltending of the man who at the time had posted the most shutouts and wins in NHL history—Sawchuk—and now I've won three Cups as a scout thanks to the man who bettered those records in Marty. Martin has the old drive, the strong will to win, just like Terry did. Both won the Calder Trophy in their rookie season and own several Vezina Trophies. And like Terry, who is the only goalie ever to beat the Canadiens in two Stanley Cup finals, Marty has also owned Montreal. His 38 career wins against the Canadiens are the most ever by a Quebec-born goalie. Brodeur is also 4-1 against Montreal in playoff action.

He's got all the records. When he's done, he's going to go down in history as one of the greatest goalies in the history of the game. And like Terry, I can call him a good friend. We hit it off right away. He's such an easy-going, humble man.

With New Jersey, our success story starts at the top, where Lamoriello has been GM since 1987. There's a lot of stability. Our scouting staff has been together as long as I've been there. David Conte has been with the team for 27 years and Claude Carrier, Conte's assistant, has worked for the franchise since 1984. In fact, all of the scouts with the team when New Jersey won its first Stanley Cup in 1995—Conte, Carrier, Dan Labraaten, Milt Fisher and me—are still part of the staff.

I was very much a team player when I played, and I enjoy my job as a scout with the Devils for much the same reason as I enjoyed playing. We're as much a team as the guys on the ice. It's a team game and you have to play as a team, and it's the same thing with scouting, you have to scout as a team. We have good cooperation between all the scouts.

Our draft strategy is similar to the Devils' on-ice game plan—unselfish and methodical. Teamwork is emphasized. The scouting staff meets with Conte and Carrier before the draft. Each scout lobbies for players in his area he feels are must-haves. When we meet before the draft, we go around the table and each scout makes the case for the players he likes. There are never any arguments between us, just statements of facts. This straightforward approach continues once the proceedings commence on draft day. We draft kids that we know are going to fit our

system. You get to figure out the players that you like, and then you can identify with them.

We don't work the same way as other teams. We collectively agree on a list of players and stay to it. We draw up that list of names and stick to that list religiously, placing stock in character. The player at the top of that list when it's our turn to make a selection is the player that will be selected. We take the best hockey player. If we need a right-winger, but we feel the best player there is a centre, we take the centre. The first three rounds, we take the best player. After that, we try to fill our holes.

When I'm scouting—let's say I'm going to Quebec to check out some draft-eligible players—here's how our system works. The Quebec scout has pulled out what he thinks are prospects, so he wants to see if I can do the same. The way we work, we have five different scouts go there to watch different hockey games, five sets of eyes to check things out. The more games you have by different people, the truer the picture you get. We put all that in the computer, and our chief scout goes through the computer and tabulates it. We don't exchange names amongst ourselves.

We like to rate all the players each and every game they play. We take note of the importance

183

of the game and who players are playing against and who is checking them. I like to look at all the players, including the players who have already been drafted by other teams. You never know if your general manager is going to make a deal for another team's prospect and if he comes to you before making the deal, you'd better have a good read on that player.

While picking out players I like, I have my own set of guidelines. I evaluate all players differently depending on the style of game they play, looking at each players' skating, hands, courage, physical play and hockey sense. I base it on past experience, people I played with and played against. I ask who a player reminds me of. Then I ask another question—if I was to play in the same league, would I like to have a guy to play with or for me, or would I love to play against him? If I'd love to play against him, I don't want him.

I have a mini Stanley Cup for each of my eight championships. For a while, after we'd moved into our new home, I only had the 2000 Cup on display because most of my stuff was packed away until I built my little museum downstairs. Now it's all set up and I have a

The rewards for all of that hard work. My miniature Stanley Cups.

mini Cup for every day of the week and two on Sunday. There's something different about each Cup. Each one is special in its own way.

The 2003 Cup win over Anaheim, for example, was a record-setter for me. It came 53 years after my first Stanley Cup win as a player with Detroit in 1950, and that 53-year difference from my first to most recent inscription on the trophy is a Stanley Cup record.

Winning the Cup as a scout, it's a different form of pride than when you achieve something with a team as a player, but it's a prideful feeling just the same. You're the one who found those guys. Some you recommended and some you didn't. It's gratifying, but I never forget that I wasn't the only one who made a contribution to the team.

I've always enjoyed winning a title because it was a group effort that made the achievement possible. I'm not really the type of person who focuses on individual recognition, but I have had my fair share of that sort of thing come my way and I have felt honoured by every instance.

In 1995, I was inducted into the Windsor Essex County Sports Hall of Fame and I have to admit, at first, I was a little concerned about making a speech at the banquet. I was thinking that if I were to take time to thank

everyone deserving of recognition we'd be there all night. Getting to that Hall of Fame, this was a real honour for me and I have to admit, it kind of caught me by surprise. I've always felt that Windsor is my adopted city. I think the town you play junior in always kind of becomes your second home. You're taken in by a family and treated like one of their own and the whole town gets to know who you are. Windsor became my family's home when I played for the Red Wings and my children attended school there. Windsor is a blue-collar town and the town I'm from is also a blue-collar town. I guess that's why I've always felt at home in Windsor.

A decade later, the Spitfires recognized my contribution to the franchise by honouring the No. 4 sweater that I'd worn while a member of the team. It's funny, because Windsor was really the only place where I didn't wear No. 3. In Omaha, they gave me No. 3. When I was called up to Indianapolis, I wore No. 3. Although I didn't start with No. 3 in Detroit, when Bill Quackenbush was traded to Boston I took his No. 3 sweater, mainly because it gave me a larger lower berth on the train trips, which were assigned by sweater numbers. After I was dealt to Toronto, I wore No. 3. In fact, in my last full

185

season as a Leaf, we acquired Pierre Pilote from Chicago. He was another future Hall of Fame defenceman and he wore No. 3 his whole career in Chicago, but in Toronto, he was relegated to No. 2 because I already had No. 3 on my back.

The Spitfires also invited me to be part of the closing ceremonies at Windsor Arena on December 4, 2008 as the team played its last game at the old barn prior to moving into the new WFCU Centre. I'd also been there in 1975, when the club played its first game back in the league. Between playing, coaching and scouting, I doubt that anyone has seen more games in that rink than me. I still get chills when I walk into Windsor Arena. There are a lot of memories for me in that place, especially upstairs, because that's where our dressing room was. That's where it all really started for me, my life in hockey. I don't get too emotional, but in each of these cases, the gesture was appreciated.

In 2012, I was inducted into the Michigan Sports Hall of Fame and in 2009, I was given recognition of a different kind by the Red Wings, my first NHL team. I received a package from the team and when UPS called to see if they could deliver it, they wanted to know if I was a jewellery dealer because of the value placed on it. It was a championship ring from

The Ilitch family presented me this Stanley Cup ring in 2009.

the Red Wings, along with a personal note of thanks from the owners of the team, Mike and Marian Ilitch. It was their idea—and what a class gesture it was—to send rings to each of the players who'd won Cups with the organization prior to 1997. I was really shocked by this. It was a grand gesture and I called Mr. Ilitch to thank him. I was so proud I took it to the OHL All-Star Game and showed it to everyone.

Receiving that ring led me to think back to those teams. We didn't receive Stanley Cup rings in the 1950s. It just wasn't part of the tradition back then. The first ring I ever got from a team was when I won the cup with Toronto in

186

1967. The one from Toronto isn't nearly the size of the Detroit ring. Toronto won four Stanley Cups during the 1960s and in those days, the Maple Leafs kept using the same ring over and over, they just made the diamond bigger for each cup you won. I also have three championship rings from my time as a scout from the Devils, but this Detroit ring completed my collection. I was raised by Detroit in their farm system. It's nice how they recognize their history.

When it comes to emotional moments, it's difficult to top the night in 1978 when I was inducted into the Hockey Hall of Fame. I was amazed. I never thought I deserved it. And I went in the same year as my old midget teammate Jacques Plante, which was really something. But most importantly of all, my mom and dad were there and they saw it. That meant a lot to me.

You don't get anywhere in this game without the love and support of a strong family. It's your parents who make the sacrifice of time and money to get you the gear and cover the costs of ice time when you are playing youth hockey.

My good friend, sportswriter Jacques Beauchamp, introduced me at my Hockey Hall of Fame induction ceremony in 1978.

Some days, I still find it hard to believe that I'm in the Hockey Hall of Fame.

Cindy and I are flanked by my parents Leo and Juliette on our wedding day in Shawinigan.

188

Once you make it to the pros, it's your wife and children who make the sacrifices as you spend so much time away travelling from city to city.

I met my wife Cindy for the first time when I was playing fastball in the summer in Shawinigan for a team called Fraser Grace. I was the catcher. I would go home in the off season from playing for the Red Wings and play ball. Her brother was on the team, so our meeting was just a coincidence. We went for a coffee after a game and we hit it off right away. We were married in 1951.

I started playing junior in Windsor and knew the city well, so I figured it would be a good place to live. We thought it would be a good place to raise our children. We had three children, two sons and a daughter. Michel is our oldest, followed by Brigitte and Leo. Cindy was a big part of my playing career. She had input into all of our decisions. When I was traded Toronto in 1965, we talked about whether going there after all those years in Detroit would be a good idea. Likewise, she sat in on my meetings with Maple Leafs GM Jim Gregory when he offered me the coaching position in Tulsa in 1970. She wasn't going to okay the move until we were certain that there were neighbourhoods and schools suitable for raising our children.

I lost my wife Cindy after 42 years of marriage in 1993 when she passed away after battling cancer. I met my second wife Eva and we were married in 1994. She's been a huge help to me as I've battled with my own share of illness in recent years—a stroke that I suffered in 1999 and a more recent fight with bladder cancer in 2012.

When I suffered the stroke, at first, my right arm didn't belong to me. It dragged behind me. I couldn't write my name. The simplest things became an ordeal—washing myself, brushing my teeth, shaving, even eating a bowl of cereal. I had to think about every move I made just to put on a shirt.

It scared the hell out of me. I thought, "What if this had happened at training camp? If I had been in a hotel, I wouldn't have been able to do anything. Who would hear me?" I had lost my ability to speak. I wouldn't have been

My second wife Eva and I pose with the Stanley Cup at the 2000 NHL entry draft in Calgary, shortly after I'd won my second Stanley Cup as a scout with the Devils.

able to yell out and call for help. It was frightening to think about what might have been.

I'm a stubborn man, though, and I worked hard to get back on track. I guess I have good genes, because I was able to get back to where I was. I was lucky then, and I was lucky again when I won my fight with cancer. I was declared cancer-free by my doctors in June of 2012.

Experiences like that, they humble you. You learn to prize what you have and appreciate the support you get from your family. Eva

190

This photo is from a Christmas card we received from Devils owner John McMullen after our 2000 Stanley Cup victory. That's his dog Bubba posing next to Lord Stanley's mug.

has been there for me through all of this. She's the one who makes sure I stay on the straight and narrow and get to all my appointments. She takes care of me. I'm a lucky man and I count my blessings for that.

In both instances, the Devils have allowed me the time to recuperate and get healthy again. But you always miss the game. I remember coercing a fellow scout to drive me to Kalamazoo while I was recovering from my stroke to check out a college defenceman we had our eye on back then. Then I talked another scout into taking me to an OHL game in Plymouth. Like I said, once hockey is in your blood, there's no transfusion that can ever remove it.

People ask me all the time about the differences between the game as I played it and how it is played today. I think we had more respect for each other. I like the game now, but I wouldn't want to play it. Still, I think it's funny when people tell me the game has changed. The game hasn't changed, the kids have. Kids today are bigger and better coached than in my day, but the one thing I like to tell them is to not be afraid of a little extra work.

One element that hasn't changed—you'd better be able to skate. If you can't skate, then you'd better have extra-great hands or be the toughest SOB in the game. And if you want to win, you better have what it takes inside your heart and your guts. That's where winning comes from.

It seems like I've been on the road my whole life, but it's been a lifetime in the game and I wouldn't trade my time in hockey for any other job in the world. Working with Lou Lamoriello has been so enjoyable. He's such a competent man and he's very loyal to his employees. At my age, I have slowed down a bit and the Devils, they have allowed me to do that. When I was younger, it was nothing to do a game, travel 100 miles and do another game.

My goal was to play in the NHL and I did for 21 years. Coaching and scouting have kept me in the game for over six decades. I've made pretty good money with the Devils. I'll stay with New Jersey as long as they want me. When I talk to Lou, he says, "It's up to you. When you quit, you quit. That's fine. But you don't have to quit."

I've had fun. And I'm still having fun. I look back and I thank the good Lord every day. Hockey has given me everything I have and I'm grateful for that.

191

New Jersey director of scouting David Conte on Marcel: "We've been very fortunate and the guys who deserve most of the credit are our scouts like Claude Carrier, Dan Labraaten and Marcel Pronovost."

Longest-Tenured NHL Teammates

Players	Team	Seasons
Gordie Howe-Alex Delvecchio	Detroit Red Wings	21 (1950-51-1970-71)
Tim Horton-George Armstrong	Toronto Maple Leafs	19 (1951-52-1969-70)
Marcel Pronovost-Gordie Howe	Detroit Red Wings	16 (1949-50-1964-65)
Henri Richard-Jean Beliveau	Montreal Canadiens	16 (1955-56-1970-71)
Bob Gainey-Larry Robinson	Montreal Canadiens	16 (1973-74-1988-89)
Rod Gilbert-Jean Ratelle	New York Rangers	16 (1960-61-1975-76)

Longest Tenure in Professional Hockey*

	Years
Marcel Pronovost	65
King Clancy	64
Jack Adams	59
Gordie Howe	58
Hap Emms	57
Harry Howell	55
Brian Kilrea	55
Art Ross	54

*As player, coach, general manager or scout

This is why we all played the game—to hold the Stanley Cup.

Some of my championship rings, including the ring we got in Belle River for the OHA Jr C Championship in 1985.

My wife Cindy clips out some articles about me while I look on.

MARCEL PRONOVOST STATISTICS

Player Stats
Regular Season

Season	Team	League	GP	G	A	P	PM
1947-48	Detroit Auto Club	IAHL	19	5	3	8	53
1947-48	Windsor Spitfires	JOHA	33	6	18	24	61
1948-49	Windsor Spitfires	JOHA	42	14	21	35	134
1948-49	Detroit Auto Club	IAHL	9	4	4	8	24
1949-50	Omaha Knights	USHL	69	13	39	52	100
1950-51	Indianapolis Capitols	AHL	34	9	23	32	44
1950-51	Detroit Red Wings	NHL	37	1	6	7	20
1951-52	Detroit Red Wings	NHL	69	7	11	18	50
1952-53	Detroit Red Wings	NHL	68	8	19	27	72
1953-54	Detroit Red Wings	NHL	57	6	12	18	50
1954-55	Detroit Red Wings	NHL	70	9	25	34	90
1955-56	Detroit Red Wings	NHL	68	4	13	17	46
1956-57	Detroit Red Wings	NHL	70	7	9	16	38
1957-58	Detroit Red Wings	NHL	62	2	18	20	52
1958-59	Detroit Red Wings	NHL	69	11	21	32	44
1959-60	Detroit Red Wings	NHL	69	7	17	24	38
1960-61	Detroit Red Wings	NHL	70	6	11	17	44

1961-62	Detroit Red Wings	NHL	70	4	14	18	38
1962-63	Detroit Red Wings	NHL	69	4	9	13	48
1963-64	Detroit Red Wings	NHL	67	3	17	20	42
1964-65	Detroit Red Wings	NHL	68	1	15	16	45
1965-66	Toronto Maple Leafs	NHL	54	2	8	10	34
1966-67	Toronto Maple Leafs	NHL	58	2	12	14	28
1967-68	Toronto Maple Leafs	NHL	70	3	17	20	48
1968-69	Toronto Maple Leafs	NHL	34	1	2	3	20
1969-70	Toronto Maple Leafs	NHL	7	0	1	1	4
1969-70	Tulsa Oilers	CHL	53	1	16	17	24
1970-71	Tulsa Oilers	CHL	17	0	0	0	4
NHL Totals			1206	88	257	345	851
Totals			1482	140	381	521	1295

Playoffs

Season	Team	League	GP	G	A	P	PM
1947-48	Windsor Spitfires	JOHA	12	1	3	4	28
1948-49	Windsor Spitfires	JOHA	4	1	5	6	2
1948-49	Detroit Auto Club	IAHL	6	3	1	4	15
1948-49	Windsor Hettche Spitfires	IAHL	5	1	4	5	13
1949-50	Omaha Knights	USHL	7	4	9	13	9
1949-50	Detroit Red Wings	NHL	9	0	1	1	10
1950-51	Detroit Red Wings	NHL	6	0	0	0	0
1951-52	Detroit Red Wings	NHL	8	0	1	1	10
1952-53	Detroit Red Wings	NHL	6	0	0	0	6
1953-54	Detroit Red Wings	NHL	12	2	3	5	12
1954-55	Detroit Red Wings	NHL	11	1	2	3	6
1955-56	Detroit Red Wings	NHL	10	0	2	2	8

1956-57	Detroit Red Wings	NHL	5	0	0	0	6
1957-58	Detroit Red Wings	NHL	4	0	1	1	4
1959-60	Detroit Red Wings	NHL	6	1	1	2	2
1960-61	Detroit Red Wings	NHL	9	2	3	5	0
1962-63	Detroit Red Wings	NHL	11	1	4	5	8
1963-64	Detroit Red Wings	NHL	14	0	2	2	14
1964-65	Detroit Red Wings	NHL	7	0	3	3	4
1965-66	Toronto Maple Leafs	NHL	4	0	0	0	6
1966-67	Toronto Maple Leafs	NHL	12	1	0	1	8
1969-70	Tulsa Oilers	CHL	2	0	0	0	0
Stanley Cup Totals			134	8	23	31	104
Totals			170	18	45	63	171

Coaching Stats
Regular Season

Season	Team	League	GP	W	L	T	FINISH
1969-70	Tulsa Oilers	CHL	72	35	27	10	3rd
1970-71	Tulsa Oilers	CHL	72	27	37	8	6th
1971-72	Tulsa Oilers	CHL	72	34	30	8	2nd
1972-73	Chicago Cougars	WHA	78	26	50	2	6th West
1975-76	Hull Festivals	QMJHL	57	24	26	7	4th West
1976-77	Hull Olympiques	QMJHL	72	26	37	9	5th Lebel
1977-78	Buffalo Sabres	NHL	80	44	19	17	2nd Adams
1978-79	Buffalo Sabres	NHL	24	8	10	6	-
1978-79	Hull Olympiques	QMJHL	36	4	29	3	5th Lebel
1979-80	Hull Olympiques	QMJHL	64	21	33	10	-
1981-82	Windsor Spitfires	OHL	68	22	42	4	6th Emms

			GP	W	L	T	
1982-83	Windsor Spitfires	OHL	15	2	13	0	-
1984-85	Belle River Canadiens	GLJHL	40	27	9	4	1st
NHL Totals			104	52	29	23	
WHA Totals			78	26	50	2	
Totals			750	300	362	88	

Playoffs

Season	Team	League	GP	W	L	RESULT
1969-70	Tulsa Oilers	CHL	6	2	4	LSF
1971-72	Tulsa Oilers	CHL	13	6	7	LF
1975-76	Hull Festivals	QMJHL	6	2	4	LQF
1976-77	Hull Olympiques	QMJHL	4	0	4	LQF
1977-78	Buffalo Sabres	NHL	8	3	5	LQF
1981-82	Windsor Spitfires	OHL	9	3	6	LQF
1984-85	Belle River Canadiens	GLJHL	28	23	5	WC
Stanley Cup Totals			8	3	5	
Totals			74	39	35	

Legend: A—Assists; AHL—American Hockey League; CHL—Central Hockey League; G—Goals; GLJHL—Great Lakes Junior C Hockey League; GP—Games Played; JOHA—Ontario Hockey Association Junior A Series; L—Lost; LF—Lost Final; IAHL—International Amateur Hockey League; LQF—Lost Quarter-final; LSF—Lost Semifinal; NHL—National Hockey League; OHL—Ontario Hockey League; P—Points; PIM—Penalties In Minutes; QMJHL—Quebec Major Junior Hockey League; T—Tied; USHL—United States Hockey League; W—Won; WC—Won Championship; WHA—World Hockey Association.